THE HOW-TO BOOK
OF
HYPNOTISM

Hypnotically
How To D

GW00778082

ORMOND McGILL, Ph.D.
and
TOM SILVER, C.Ht.

The Silver Institute Publishing Co.
Newbury Park, California

Printed in the United States of America

First Printed Edition: January 2000
Second Printing: February 2001
Third Printing: July 2002

Published by:
The Silver Institute Publishing Co.
P.O. Box 189
Newbury Park, CA 91319-0189
1-888-646-3797
www.tomsilver.com

TABLE OF CONTENTS

- As a Hypnotic Experiment
- Suggestion in Salesmanship
- Suggestion Changes Opinions
- Suggestion for Health
- Suggestion in the Home
- Suggestion in the School
- Increasing the Power of Suggestions

CHAPTER TEN (cont.)
- Cannot Get Up
- Making the Subject Follow You
- Cannot Jump Over A Stick
- Cannot Speak His Name
- Cannot Open His Eyes
- Suggestions for Different Tests

INFLUENCING A NUMBER OF PEOPLE AT THE SAME TIME WITH WAKING HYPNOSIS
- The Rotating Hands
- The Slapping Thighs
- The Shaking Hands
- The Missing Fingertips

HOW TO INDUCE HYPNOTIC SLEEP
- The Test of Hypnotic Sleep
- Posthypnosis
- Awakening the Subject

OTHER METHODS OF INDUCING HYPNOTIC SLEEP
- The Sydney Flower Method
- Hypnotizing by Telephone
- Hypnotizing by Mail
- The Mesmeric Method

INSTANTANEOUS METHODS OF HYPNOTIZING
- The Eye Closure Method
- The Sudden Sleep Method
- The Chair "Bump" Method

LIST OF ILLUSTRATIONS

NOTE TO THE READER

This book is intended for mature readers, 18 years of age or older. It is an introduction to the science of hypnotism and the reader is advised to use caution and good judgement when conducting hypnosis demonstrations or exercises. The authors also advise that hypnosis demonstrations and hypnotic inductions be conducted under the guidance of a trained clinical hypnotherapist. An education in hypnosis through a clinical hypnotherapy training center is also advised. Anyone reading this book is advised *under no circumstances* to have subjects perform any demonstrations that might be detrimental to their physical or mental well-being.

The Silver Hypnosis Institute

Just off the press is a brand new book written by Tom Silver and Ormond McGill that will teach you everything that you need to know to be a great Hypnotherapist:

"HYPNOTISM"
THE REAL QUESTIONS AND ANSWERS OF HYPNOSIS
"A Hypnosis Training and Techniques Manual" which includes 130 Questions and Answers of Hypnosis and Hypnosis Induction Techniques, Suggestions and Visual Imagery Techniques and more! This book gives the reader an abundance of knowledge and techniques to make you a great Hypnotherapist"
ISBN # 0-9678515-9-9

NOTE FROM THE AUTHORS

Hypnotism and its associated professional practice of hypnotherapy is our way of life. In this book, we tell of this age old science and art, past, present, and future, in the hope that we may share our knowledge and love of hypnosis to you, the reader.

Ormond McGill & Tom Silver
Clinical Hypnotherapists
California, USA
January 2000

INTRODUCTION

Interest in hypnotism is sweeping the world. Demonstrations are being exhibited and numerous schools of training in hypnotherapy can be found in every major city. This interest is natural. We are advancing ever deeper into the realm of computer technology and the human brain is the greatest computer of all. Hypnotism provides a means of programming our very personal inner computer. Hypnosis provides a wonderful key for unlocking our mental "wonderhouse".

This book is a "How-To" instructional manual of how to hypnotize, how to demonstrate hypnotic phenomena and how to use hypnosis for many useful purposes.

Hypnotism is a very practical psychology. Mankind's knowledge advances by spreading knowledge. No study is more important than the advancement of the human mind, our greatest gift.

Stage demonstrations of hypnotism have brought it to the attention of many people who would otherwise have missed an appreciation of this remarkable science/art. As a therapeutic agent, hypnotism stands supreme. The hypnotist is always ready to serve humanity. The value of hypnotherapy gains recognition on a daily basis throughout the world. Its value will continue to advance greatly as mankind comes to understand and learn how to operate the remarkable biocomputer that lies inside our heads.

Hypnosis provides the means of programming your mental computer. This volume is a "How-To" text of hypnotism. It presents step-by-step instructions so that you will learn with ease and enjoyment. " For we learn best that which we enjoy learning."

Ormond McGill & Tom Silver performing a "two-man" hypnosis show.
Stanford University, Palo Alto, California. May 1999

Tom Silver standing next to a Buddhist Temple
on the side of a cliff overlooking the coast of Taiwan.
Behind the Temple, inside the rock cliff, is a Shaman Healers
cave/office, where the ancient art of Shamanism healing takes place.

CHAPTER ONE

A HISTORY OF HYPNOTISM

Hypnotism in one form or another has been practiced for a very long time. For hundreds of years the Yogi have applied the practice in various ways. They would throw themselves and others into a trance state of mind through concentration on various mantras.

Hypnotic phenomena can be observed in the ancient practices of Egyptian priests used in Temples of Healing. Also, the Persian Magi and Chinese Mystics used it to alleviate suffering.

The psychic side of hypnotism, such as clairvoyance and mental telepathy (which today is referred to as ESP) were also recorded among the old forms of hypnotism. We read of such references in relation to the Hebrew prophecies and the Oracles of Greece. Those who practiced such strange and secret powers were held in awe by the ancients. Little wonder, as the secrets were kept closely guarded and were passed on by word of mouth only among the elect. That is to say, handed on from father to son as a precious heritage.

With the advent of Jesus Christ, an avenue of enlightenment was opened. He told of such truths about the wonderful inner nature of man. This Master performed miracles through the power of the mind. He explained that they were miracles that all could perform. He willingly revealed these divine secrets which cured people of many ailments. He even resurrected the dead by His hypnotic and occult power, which was manifested by suggestion and the laying on of hands. The masses, with few exceptions, were not ready to mentally grasp the principles of His teachings and preferred to stay in ignorance and superstition. However, the seed was sown, and it could not entirely be destroyed even by His death. His twelve Apostles carried on His work and spread His teachings among many nations. Today His doctrines and followers number in the billions.

We find a large number of mental healers among the early Christians who applied Christ's methods of curing the sick. They were persecuted by the Romans and then put to death. The result was that after a time, in that period of early history, such methods of healing (the laying on of hands and prayer mantras of suggestive therapy) almost became obliterated. However, with the later rise of Christian Churches, numerous priests and monks returned to faith healing and the suggestive power of prayer.

In the later part of the 18th Century, a Jesuit Priest by the name of Father Gassner created a sensation in Germany. He would induce the hypnotic condition by suddenly entering a room where a person was waiting and, with an uplifted crucifix in one hand, walk towards the person to call out in a Stentorian voice the word "sleep" in Latin. Invariably he would thus induce a state of hypnosis. He performed some remarkable experiments. In one of his "sensitives" he suspended the heartbeat for several minutes and then called the person back to life after an apparent death.

Another 18th Century man who was instrumental in renewed interest in this subject was the Viennese physician, Dr. Frederick Anton Mesmer, who is credited with being the "father" of mental medicine in relatively modern times.

Mesmer came to Paris in the Spring of 1778 from Vienna, Austria where he had obtained his original degree. From working with physical magnets, (which was popular with doctors of the period) he developed a theory of using his hands for curing, stating that they exuded the same magnetic influence as a physical magnet. As this influence was organic in nature, he called it "Animal Magnetism". He claimed that this magnetism was in the human body and could be communicated from doctor to patient. He performed remarkable cures and his process became known as "Mesmerism".

Paris received Mesmer and his doctrines with open arms. He soon opened one of the finest salons imaginable where he treated and cured hundreds of people, rich and poor alike. The demand for his treatments became so great that he conceived the idea of treating his patients "en masse". He installed a sort of fountain in the center of his treatment room, which was called the "baquet". It was filled with water which had been previously "magnetized". The "baquet" was then covered with a lid which had holes in it and through these holes, iron rods protruded (one for each patient). Thirty or so patients could be treated simultaneously while seated around the contrivance. Mesmer was dressed in a lilac robe while music played in the background. He would walk around and touch each patient's troubled part of the body, while the patients held the energy rod from the baquet. Also, the patients were tied together by a silver cord. Hundreds of cures are on record, which he accomplished by this procedure. It is recorded that he treated over 8,000 patients during the year of 1784. It has been said that he charged exorbitant fees for his services and that he made a fortune for himself. This is true in regards to his rich patrons, but it is equally true that the poor were treated similarly yet free of charge.

His success aroused the jealous antagonism of other French physicians who discredited his work. Mesmer returned to his native country where he died in 1815.

Following Mesmer, the next historic figure who was prominent in the advancement of hypnotherapeutics was Dr. James Braid of England.

Dr. Braid was born in 1795 in Edinburgh. He graduated there as a physician and surgeon. He settled in Manchester after practicing medicine in Scotland for a number of years and remained there until his death in 1860. Dr. Braid is regarded as the real rediscoverer of what is today called "hypnotism". In fact, it was he who coined that name. He took it from the Greek word "Hypnos", which means the god of sleep. Thus, "hypnotism", as we know it today, was born.

After having witnessed an exhibition on mesmerism and animal magnetism presented by a French mesmerist in the city of Manchester, England, Dr. Braid started a series of experiments on his own. He soon found that the same phenomena could be produced without using passes and without need for a belief in a so called "magnetic fluid". He developed a method of having his subjects gaze intently at a bright object held some inches in front of and above the eyes which seemed to produce a state analogous to natural sleep. His method seeded to produce results similar to those claimed by the mesmerists. Braid concluded that "animal magnetism" had nothing to do with the production of the phenomena. In his opinion, it was a matter of the concentration of the subject upon the object held in front of his eyes. In his early work he used no verbal suggestions to amplify the trance state. In later years, Dr. Braid added suggestions to his technique. As was mentioned, he called the mental condition he induced "hypnotism" and the termination of the condition he called "dehypnotizing".

His conscientious work in the field led other prominent men of his times to study the phenomena, which advanced an understanding of its psychological nature. Among these was Dr. A.A. Liebault of France.

In 1864 Dr. Liebault settled in Nancy, France to practice medicine and hypnotism. His hypnotic patients grew so numerous that he was forced to enlarge his quarters. His successful work with hypnotism soon attracted attention throughout France. Subsequently he joined forces with his esteemed physician friend, Dr. Bernheim, and together the Nancy School of Hypnotherapy was formed.

4

Liebault used Braid's method of inducing hypnotic sleep using verbal suggestions along with it at all times. The value of suggestions was recognized by himself and Bernheim. They published an acclaimed work titled "Suggestive Therapeutics" some years later which was based on case histories of cures performed at their "Nancy Clinic."

At this same historic period, Dr. Charcot in the Sapetriere of Paris drew attention to the subject and attracted many followers. The Sapetriere and the Nancy School held many differences of opinions about the causation of hypnotic phenomena. Charcot asserted that only neurotic and hysterical people could be hypnotized. The Nancy School held that induced somnambulism (hypnosis) is universal to all humanity and healthy people actually made the best subjects.

After the death of these pioneers in modern hypnotism, the therapeutic use of hypnosis fell in decline as Freud's work in psychoanalysis came to the forefront. During that period it was stage hypnotists touring countries who kept hypnotism publicly alive.

It was during World War II that hypnosis again became revived for therapeutic use as an aid to help shell shocked soldiers. In that period hypnotism became officially recognized by the American Medical Association as having definite value as a form of healing art.

Since that recognition by the medical profession the advancement of hypnotherapy has been phenomenal. Today, a belief in the physiological transfer of human energy from doctor to patient (as Mesmer suggested) is given respect along with the psychological aspect of the psychology of suggestion.

In our opinion both aspects of the science have a place, while the association with hypnotism to programming the biocomputer of the human brain has had astronomical influence.

Ormond McGill, "The Dean of American Hypnotists," hypnotizing guests on "People Are Funny," television show starring Art Linkletter. 1945.

CHAPTER TWO

HYPNOTISM, WILL POWER, AND YOU

Now that you have had a rundown on a brief history of hypnotism, let's consider how learning "How To Hypnotize" can contribute to success in daily life. Let's consider its personal value to yourself. There is no better way of learning anything than by personal application.

In recognizing that hypnotism is induced through communication between people on both physiological and psychological levels by induced suggestions or commands from one person to another, while full attention is given to the process in which acceptance of the suggestions is emphasized, it becomes obvious that similar results in varying degrees can be produced in everyday communication. Indeed, it has been our finding that it is not necessary to induce trance (sleep-like and/or somnambulistic state) in a subject in order to produce hypnotic phenomena. With proper procedures it will be found that persons can be hypnotized in the waking state while fully conscious of what they are doing yet still be unable to resist the established influence. This is illustrated by the popular " Hand Locking Test", which Coue' always used in his clinic when working with patients, in which the subject's hands are fastened together so firmly by suggestion that he cannot release them from each other until the hypnotist gives the command that they will come apart when the suggestion is given for them to separate. Full directions for performing this "Hand Locking Test" will be given in a subsequent chapter.

To produce effective experiments in waking hypnosis, the operator must know how to positively direct the suggestions. The basic secret is this: the hypnotist knows how to influence the subjective (subconscious) mind of the person while the latter does not know how to resist it and as a consequence obeys the commands even when such are contrary to his conscious judgment.

Hypnotizing is not a question of a weak mind verses a strong mind. It is not a question of willpower. Becoming an expert hypnotist comes from learning how to effectively influence subconscious mind activity while bypassing conscious mind nonacceptance. Willpower comes solely as the directive aim of the hypnotist. Directive aim of the mind to accomplish anything in life is the key to success. In such regard, learning the art of hypnotizing is a key factor to success in accomplishing whatever you will yourself to accomplish. In relation to hypnosis, such can almost be likened to a direct telepathic influence of mind upon mind, while the verbalized suggestions affirm the inner mental purpose of the hypnotist is to effectively influence the subject. In a nutshell, effective hypnotizing of others comes via the hypnotist knowing with positive assurance that what he suggests will be performed by the subject.

Learning how to hypnotize automatically increases one's willpower, and willpower properly directed will cause things to come one's way with half the difficulty compared to one who does not use this remarkable mental gift.

For example, some people do things by the sheer force of will. Two merchants started in the same line of business on opposite sides of the street at the same time. Each had an equal chance to do business. Within a few years, one of them had prospered tremendously and had to build a larger store to accommodate his business. The other was still in the same little store doing about the same amount of business as when he first started. Why? The prosperous merchant had used his will to succeed, while the less successful merchant was too lazy to use his will. The successful merchant used the power within himself to attract new customers and continued to keep them. He was always alert and his mind is constantly working and influencing people to buy from him. Learning the art of hypnotism trains you in that skill.

To succeed, you will have to shake off that lazy feeling of "I wish that I could" and transform it to "I know that I can". The will can be trained by mental exercise, the same as the body can be trained by physical exercise. The development of your willpower is part of the training you will gain from this "How-To" book. Following the lessons will develop a wonderful power within you. Indeed, it may even seem like you are awakening from a long sleep. You will find yourself a changed individual at the end of this training. Every person has the same power of potential within them. All that is needed is to learn how to cultivate and use it.

Some people naturally have a magnetic personality and use that power to influence others unconsciously. It is a talent. However, it is something everyone can learn to do by training the mind in that hypnotic direction. Just follow the instructions as they are given to you in this book and you will acquire the power. It is a power beyond your wildest dreams. It will brace you up. You will walk erect. Your eyes will clear and you will look everyone head on. All shyness will vanish like a drop of water on a hot tin roof. In place of fear you will have confidence. With a mind that is positive instead of negative, you will radiate a force that is practically irresistible to the people with whom you come in contact with. This is the power you will develop as you become a hypnotist.

Of course, do not expect to influence everybody because there are some people whose magnetism is antagonistic to you, but you will be able to influence a full seventy-five percent of those you try to hypnotize. You can hardly call that percentage bad. Learning how to hypnotize is like everything else in life. Persevere. If at first you don't succeed - try, try again - and it is guaranteed you will.

9

Hypnotizing your first subject is the first hurdle you must pass. Once you have had your first success, you will advance by leaps and bounds.

Have confidence in yourself. Learn your lessons well. Practice what you learn. Persevere and as surely as the sun comes up each morning you will succeed. You will become a hypnotist.

As you learn the "How-To" of hypnotizing others it will make you a master of yourself.

Tom Silver preparing to hypnotize three different people in a grocery store all at the same time to do wild and crazy things under hypnosis for a segment on "The Montel Williams Television Show". August 1998

11

CHAPTER THREE

THE POWER OF SUGGESTION

The subconscious plays the role of supervisor over our body's physical processes. All of the vital organs are controlled by its agency: digestion, assimilation, the circulation of the blood, heartbeat, the action of the lungs, the kidneys.

The subconscious never sleeps. During sleep it seems to be more alert and active than it is during our waking hours. In the state of hypnosis suggestions become hyperpromotional.

The two aspects of the mind, conscious and subconscious, are in perpetual interaction. If we consciously think a thought and cause it to be accepted by the subconscious, the idea will spontaneously go into action in producing the effect. If it is a healthful thought, we are so much better. If it is a diseased thought, we are so much the worse. For unlike our conscious mind, the subconscious has no selective power. Whatever is presented to it is accepted and automatically acted upon. It is in the process of the transformation of a thought into an element of our life that we make use of the power of suggestion. Since the phenomena is a normal part of the mind's action, we can easily find evidence of its workings in our daily experiences.

Consider the case of a man with "stage fright". In private, he delivers his speech splendidly, but no sooner has he set foot on the public platform than his knees begin to knock, his heart hammers, his mouth becomes dry, and after a few stammering remarks, he is forced to make a hasty exit from the stage.

CHAPTER FOUR

MORE ON THE POWER OF SUGGESTION

If we can get the subconscious to accept an idea, realization follows automatically. For any idea to enter the subconscious it must be charged with emotion. This is where so many of the "thinking fads" fall down. For it is not the thinking of ideas that is of paramount importance, but rather it is the emotional drive that is given to the idea being thought about.

For such reasons ideas that are directly associated to our personal experience are the ones most likely to carry the greatest suggestive influence. Ideas relating to health, pain, success, or a goal dear to our hearts all carry an emotional impact. The greater the operation of the power of suggestion.

The ready acceptance or rejection of an idea by the subconscious depends largely on the associations connected with it. Thus, an idea is most readily accepted when it ties in with similar emotionally charged ideas already seated within the mind. It is rejected when it is contrary to ideas previously established. This brings us to another operating law of the Power of Suggestion:

A suggestion is accepted when it is not countered by other suggestions already established in the mind.

Such being the case, how is it possible to alter ideas already established in the subconscious?

On this point, consider the subconscious as a tide which ebbs and flows. In sleep it seems to submerge consciousness altogether, while at moments of full wakefulness the tide is at its lowest. Between these two extremes are any number of intermediary levels. When we are drowsy, dreamy, lulled into a gentle reverie by music, etc., the subconscious tide is high. While the more wakeful we become, the more it ebbs. This submergence of consciousness is referred to as the "outcropping of the subconscious."

This outcropping of the subconscious occurs in daily life most markedly in periods just before we fall to sleep and just after we wake up. But it occurs to the greatest extent of all in the hypnotic state of mind, which has the advantage of being able to cause it to occur at any time when hypnosis is induced.

During these periods of the outcropping of the sub-conscious are the times in which to effectively implant suggestions, in relation to hypnotherapeutic benefits to the subject, such as in removing unwanted habits and estab-lishing desired ones. During such periods, contrary associations do not seem to take place and established patterns in the mind lose their strength to resist change via the influx of new and desired suggestions. The power of hypnotically inspired suggestions is such that inrooted, unwanted ideas may be weeded out from the soil of mind and fresh ones planted, so that on the return to normal consciousness, a new plant of thought (behavior) will be growing in place of the old.

For a suggestion to carry power it must be accepted by the subconscious, and no amount of *willing* on our part will bring about the desired results; for willing only makes the conscious aspects of mind more active and submerges deeper the subconscious.

A person trying to use his will to implant ideas in his subconscious is attempting the impossible. A sick man tries consciously to think he is not sick, and he still remains sick. Indeed, often instead of feeling better he feels worse, for the ideas only serve to bring him to a fuller realization that he is sick. Consequently he finds himself contemplating the exact

14

opposite of what he desires. He battles with his will to repress the aroused thoughts of illness but it seems the more he tries to repress them, the more the unwanted ideas possess him. Which brings us to another basic law in the operation of the power of suggestion:

Whenever the will is in conflict with an idea, the idea invariably wins the struggle.

You can prove this principle for yourself by a little experiment:

Take a plank of wood, about six inches wide and twelve feet long, and place it on the floor of your room. Now try walking along that plank from one end to the other. Narrow as it is, you can do it easily. Next, take that same plank and place it over the canyon between two high buildings and try walking over it. You take a few timid steps out upon it and unless you make a hasty retreat your life is in danger as you would soon lose your balance and fall into the depths below.

Why?

The new position of the plank has aroused in your mind the suggestion of the idea of falling, and this idea is colored with the emotion accompanying such a possibility. Immediately your subconscious goes into operation and accepts the idea of a fall. With your will you try to battle against the impulse to fall. After all you have just walked over that very same plank in perfect safety in your room. But reason about it as you will, the more you think about not falling, the more the counter-idea that you will fall is aroused, until were you to stubbornly persist in taking the risk, you would lose your balance and topple off into space.

Thus it will be recognized, willpower is incapable of mastering subconscious power for as fast as will brings up its big guns, thought captures them and turns them against itself. This is known as the Law of Reverse Effort, viz.:

When the imagination and the will are in conflict, the imagination invariably gains the day.

The conflict between the will and the imagination is in direct ratio to the square of the will.

Thus, the will turns out to be not the commanding monarch of life, as many people would have it, but a blind Samson capable of either turning the mill or pulling down the pillars.

Using hypnosis, mastery between ideas and our will is obtained. Wrong thought can be replaced by right thoughts, not by resisting the unwanted thoughts but by overcoming (overpowering) the unwanted by the wanted. This in no way devalues "willpower"; it merely relegates it to its proper place. Will is under the direction of conscious mind and it must be used in accordance to its capacities, i.e., it can locate ideas that are unwanted; it can locate thoughts that are needed; it can direct the deliberate process that will result in the removal of the undesired and replace same with the desired, but always remember that the actual performance of the process takes place as a subconscious operation and not a conscious one. And hypnosis is the key to deliberately directing the subconscious.

Hypnosis provides our gardening tools for the successful cultivation of the fertile field of the subconscious to raise a full crop of living life as we desire it to be.

LOOK INTO MY EYES

CHAPTER FIVE

VARIOUS APPLICATIONS OF SUGGESTION

As a hypnotic experiment, have a person look at the photograph of a person with outstanding eyes and give the suggestion that by constantly looking at those eyes, the eyes will hypnotize them with an uncanny feeling resulting. Continued contemplation of the eyes with the mind centered on being hypnotized by the eyes leads to a state of mind productive of hypnosis.

The effect is increased if an outside person insistently gives suggestions (at the same time as the looking) that the eyes in the photograph will produce hypnotic effects upon the individual. In other words, while in reality it is only a photograph, the power of suggestion endows the eyes in the photograph with the power to hypnotize. The power of the suggestion is increased even more by stating that the photograph being looked at is of a famous hypnotist whose eyes have a remarkable ability to induce hypnosis.

The power of suggestion is essential to human life. It can be the foundation of success or failure. A suggestion properly given creates expectancy in the mind to such an extent that if repeated often enough, it is finally accepted as true.

SUGGESTIONS IN SALESMANSHIP

Suggestions are the essence of salesmanship. Examples are constantly in evidence. Most everyone has at sometime or other bought something they did not know they wanted yet they bought it, and it was not until later that they decided they did not want what they had been persuaded by suggestion to buy. The buying came about through the power of suggestion on the part of the person or advertisement which induced the sale.

SUGGESTION CHANGES OPINION

Frequently, people change their opinions regarding certain matters when new ideas are suggested to them. The remark, "Well, now that you speak of it, I believe it is so," is often heard. Such is directly the result of exercising the power of suggestion.

To some degree, everybody uses the power of suggestion; some consciously and some unconsciously. Some conclusively and some inconclusively. The more one knows how to deliberately use this power, the more effective is the power. Training in hypnotism brings mastery of this power to change the opinions of others.

In some persons, the use of the power of suggestion seems almost an inborn talent. They automatically use it to good effect. This is why such persons are called "natural born salesmen". Their use of the power of suggestion is naturally effectively -- it is there for the use of everyone. Used consciously in a definite direction to produce a desired result, suggestion is a limitless asset to what can be accomplished.

SUGGESTION FOR HEALTH

Suggestion can be used to help sick people get well. The value of cheerful and optimistic expression in the sick room to improve the health of an ill person is well known. The successful doctor uses the power continuously to heal his patients the fastest. It is often referred to as his "bedside manner".

Persons in all walks of life use the power. Politicians, ministers, physicians, attorneys, salesmen, actors, etc., all use the power of suggestion. The study of hypnotism trains you most effectively to use this power in all walks of life actively.

SUGGESTION IN THE HOME

Parents should know how to use the power of suggestion in bringing up and molding the character of their children. Children are very responsive to suggestion. It is foolish to inflict punishment on a child every time they do not behave or if they have acquired a bad habit. Find out who or what is responsible for suggesting such a wrong direction. For example, if a youngster comes home and starts using profanity, do not punish him. Simply take him to one side, look deep into his eyes and ask him where he heard such language. Usually it is not of his own origination; it comes via an outside source. While holding his attention, suggest that he discontinue such language. Show him the difference between right and wrong. Convince him you have his welfare as a parent in your heart, and that he cease accepting such suggestions from outside companions.

Well trained children are the result of proper suggestions on the part of their parents and teachers. In giving suggestions of behavior patterns to a child, be direct and emphatic in your suggestions, and do not change your mind as your own vacillation of ideas will confuse the child.

Learning how to give effective suggestions to the child is a must for successful parents. Some parents even take advantage of talking to the child while sleeping which directly implants suggestions of well being into the subconscious, as the natural sleep can be transformed into hypnotic sleep by careful handling. A study of hypnosis by thoughtful parents is excellent.

SUGGESTION IN THE SCHOOL

Suggestion in the field of education can be of great value. Teachers would do well to study the laws of suggestion and apply them to the classroom. A positive suggestion is like a command and it produces results automatically. It is easy to note that some teachers are far better than others. Why? Largely it is because the successful teacher knows how to appeal to the responsive minds of their students. Their teaching is in accord with irresistible suggestions of successful learning. They are magnetic and students like them. Ask a student's opinion of a teacher and you will get an "aye" or "nay". If he doesn't like him, he will not do as the teacher instructs and will learn poorly. On the other hand, if the teacher is liked by the student he will learn well.

Teachers do well to master a study of the power of suggestion.

INCREASING THE POWER OF SUGGESTIONS

There are basically two forms of hypnotic (suggestive) influence as has been previously mentioned. One is the mesmeric approach of implanting the suggestion in the subconscious through the use of human energy power. This is the mesmeric approach which was made famous as Mesmer's "Animal Magnetism". The other is the verbalized approach of using the psychological method of the power of words. Words have been conditioned in our mind to produce automatic responses. That is to say: Words are triggers to action.

The most effective form of using the power of suggestion comes through a combining of the two methods, viz.:

Form the thought within the mind first before it is spoken and think of it in terms of being directly transferred into the mind of the recipient. Then follow directly into a verbalized affirmation of the thought. Such handling greatly increases the power of suggestion and gives what you express hypnotic impact.

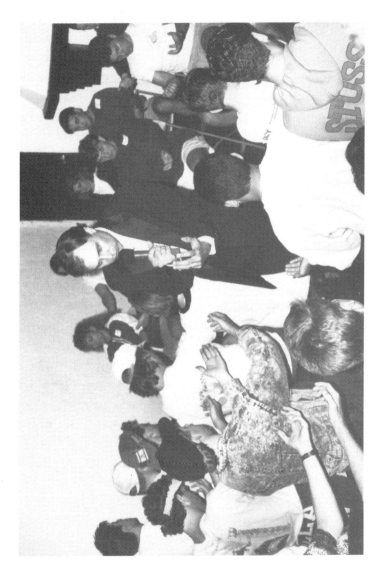

Tom hypnotizing college fraternity students at the University of California, Los Angeles (UCLA). July 1987

CHAPTER SIX

PREPARING TO BECOME A HYPNOTIST

Having learned of the Power of Suggestion, you are now ready to prepare yourself in the direction of exerting this power in a directed hypnotic way. In other words: to become a hypnotist. For a start, it is well to appreciate these fundamental facts:

ANYONE CAN MASTER HYPNOTISM

Whoever you are, whatever you are, or wherever you are, you can master the science of hypnotism. And once you learn the science, you can learn the art of its performance. Such is why hypnotism is often referred to as a science/art.

The power to hypnotize is within each person. Naturally some have more talent for it, just as some persons will have more talent than do others for singing, as an example. But the power is there inside of each and everyone to be developed. It is the purpose of this book to show you how.

Hypnotism is the foundation of all mental phenomena. The science of hypnotism is universal and has always been a part of human relationships. Each day in our current computer age the power of hypnotism is advancing. With study, the great majority of people can, in a surprisingly short time, produce results that are far beyond their expectations. This book shows you how through a very practical way of producing the phenomena instead of merely theorizing on the subject.

WHO IS HYPNOTIZABLE?

Every human being is hypnotizable to some degree or other. Twenty percent of the population are capable of entering deep hypnosis (somnambulism) on the first attempt. Others take more repeated trials. People who are mentally challenged are difficult to influence so such persons are best avoided. Quick-witted, impulsive and intelligent people make good subjects. College students and military trained personnel are excellent. Even more so are artistic and creative individuals. Working with persons between the ages of 15 and 45 is the most desirable. Children are readily hypnotized, but the state is unstable in its lasting qualities. Older persons are often so set in their ways that they resist allowing themselves to go into hypnosis.

QUALIFICATIONS OF A HYPNOTIST

The qualifications of a hypnotist are first of all confidence, a strong will, and the desire and knowledge to use both. It is not uncommon for a person to think they have a strong will because they are stubborn. Stubbornness is of no value. A strong willed person is one who knows how to direct his thoughts to accomplish the product of his thoughts. In such regard comes SELF-CONTROL. You must learn first how to control yourself before you can expect to control others. Self-control to the hypnotist means never to lose one's temper, to speak with a clear voice, have a healthy constitution, good morals and a willingness to do one's best.

One's clothes should be neat and clean, and being personally immaculate is a necessity. Show good taste in all you do and say. Do not try to convince skeptical people you can hypnotize them against their will. You must convince people to work with you in cooperation, not opposition. Never argue. Do not expect to hypnotize every person you come in contact with. Be satisfied with a fair percentage at first. Your percentage of success will increase as you advance in experience.

REQUIREMENTS FOR HYPNOSIS

The essential thing to the induction of hypnosis on the part of the subject is attention to the hypnotist's suggestions, plus a willingness to be hypnotized. Generally speaking, a person cannot be hypnotized against their conscious will, although this does not mean they cannot be hypnotized if their subconscious is willing.

Mainly, all that is necessary in a good subject is the willingness to be hypnotized, willingness to pay attention to the suggestions given by the hypnotist, and willingness to relax the physical body. In seventy-five percent of such persons you will be able to induce hypnosis in one form or another.

DEVELOPING YOUR HYPNOTIC EYES AND VOICE

It is well for the hypnotist to develop a steady and earnest gaze. If you use your eyes in hypnotizing, the less you blink your eyes the better. Getting a hypnotic gaze like this takes practice.

Just before going to bed at night, stand in front of a mirror and look steadily at your eyes. Keep your eyes from blinking for as long as you can stand it, which will be for about a minute on the first trial. The second time you practice you will be able to look longer without blinking. At first it makes your eyes smart, but this will pass in a few days as you practice developing a hypnotic gaze. Keep practicing, a bit at a time, until you can keep your gaze steady, without blinking, for up to five minutes.

Now acquire a steady eye. That is, don't let your eyes move from one point to another as most people tend to do, but when you look into the eyes of your subject, keep your gaze in a concentrated stream into their eyes.

Looking a person straight in the eyes builds immediate confidence between hypnotist and subject. The eyes have been called the "windows to the soul" or innermost consciousness. They show character, willpower, determination and strength of the individual.

It is well for the hypnotist to develop a voice that expresses self-control and power. A squeaky, uncertain voice will not present suggestions effectively. The hypnotist should speak in a pleasant, yet commanding way that automatically demands acceptance. Practice the development of your voice, just as you practiced the development of your hypnotic gaze.

Stand in front of a mirror while looking at yourself and state to your image:

"I am going to succeed and become a master hypnotist. My voice is becoming perfect to most effectively present hypnotic suggestions which will be obeyed. Day by day, in every way, my voice becomes increasingly hypnotic in what I say and the way I say it."

Learn to speak in a pleasant, even tone. Keep the pitch low. Talk to yourself as if you were conversing with a friend. It is not necessary to talk loud. Use just an ordinary tone, as in conversation. An even toned voice can accomplish wonders, whereas a jerky, squeaky voice will not make a good impression. A hypnotic voice always makes a powerful impression.

27

Learn to speak positively, in a manner that demands acceptance. Perhaps you have heard the drill sergeant tell a line of soldiers, "Attention!" Notice how he says it. It is positive. It is a command. It expects obedience. A suggestion given positively is equivalent to a command. It is speaking in a POSITIVE MANNER, and behind it is the thought that what is spoken will be followed and obeyed. Practice this positive way of speaking. For practice, you can go into your room and look at a piece of furniture and imagine it is alive - a man. Give him commands. Talk to him as if he must do and cannot refuse. Say to him:

"You WILL do as I tell you!"

"You MUST DO what I tell you!"

"You CANNOT resist me!"

Speak these phrases in a forceful manner several times over to the imaginary person. Do it seriously. Do not be afraid of being too dogmatic, as you are only practicing for yourself. Do this for at least a week once a day. Then practice the same on people you come in contact with. Naturally you will not use such dogmatic statements, but use the same commanding way. Use your will power and speak with confidence in yourself.

If you ask a person to do something for you, say to him or her, "I WISH you would do this for me." Lay emphasis on the word WISH and it will sound just like WILL. There is all the difference in the world in how this is spoken to gain immediate obedience. When spoken positively it sounds like a command. When said weakly it sounds like you are pleading.

This faculty of giving positive suggestions is essential to hypnotizing. Study and practice these instructions for

28

developing your hypnotic eyes and voice. They are important to your success as a hypnotist.

OBTAINING SUBJECTS TO PRACTICE ON

As a beginning hypnotist, you will need persons to practice with. With a little diplomacy you can easily obtain willing subjects. For this purpose, invite some congenial friends to your home who are interested in psychology. You can discuss psychology with the group without especially mentioning hypnotism at first. Turn the conversation upon the value of relaxation for removing stress from the body. You can mention that some persons who think they know how to relax really don't know how to do so. You propose a test the group can try:

Have each person in the group take a comfortable seat and give attention to the experiment you suggest. Each person is to raise his or her left arm up at a right angle out in front of his chest, then extend the forefinger of his right hand and place it directly under the palm of his left hand. In such a position, the extended finger is ready to support the entire weight of the left hand and arm.

Now tell the group to completely relax their left hand and arm -- the extended finger of the right hand being the sole support of that arm. The participants are thus in a position that requires the relaxing of the left arm while, at the same time, concentrating on holding it up with the extended forefinger of the right hand. (In this you have produced a situation requiring both concentration and relaxation at the same time -- a condition very similar to that required for the induction of hypnosis.)

Now tell the group, for each person to be sure they have relaxed their left hand and arm completely, in this testing for relaxation. At the count of "three", they are to quickly draw the right forefinger support from under the extended left hand.

You then slowly count, "*One, two, three.*" What happens? If the volunteers trying the experiment have truly relaxed as you instructed, the moment support is withdrawn from under the hand that arm naturally drops limply to their lap. Such is the expected result, but as sometimes happens, the left arm of some persons will still remain suspended even when the finger support beneath is removed.

When this happens, explain that it indicates the person has not really relaxed even when they thought they had. So repeat the experiment. A second time around most everyone will have learned to fully relax.

It is a simple experiment, but it is interesting and gets the group participating in some demonstrations with you. You can then turn the discussion to William James's effect of Ideomoter Action, that every idea of motion held in the mind produces an accompanying unconscious motor-muscular response in the body of a minute nature.

To demonstrate this, hand each person a pendulum (simply a small fishing weight tied to the end of a length of string). Instruct them to hold the top end of the string in their right hand, allowing the weight to dangle down as they hold it with arm outstretched. Tell them to think of it being still. It will become still. Now tell them to think of it swinging back and forth -- just the thought alone without making any conscious muscular effort to move it. It will begin to sway back and forth.

Next tell them to think of the pendulum swinging around and around in a circle and it will so respond. Response to this pendulum test will give you a good idea as to whom in the group is the more responsive to suggestions.

These simple experiments will quickly capture group interest and you can now proceed to trying some experiments in waking hypnosis (as you will be instructed) such as Falling Backwards and Forward Tests, Fastening Hands

Together, etc.. When you feel the group is ready for it, you can suggest trying a few experiments in hypnotism -- inducing trance.

In practicing hypnosis with your friends, it is often best not to mention hypnotism at first, but generally lead up to it. And never mention that you are a beginner and just practicing.

This initial practice with friends in experimenting with hypnotism is very important as it is desirable for you to achieve good results right from the start. To be a successful hypnotist, nothing is more important than to have confidence in your ability to hypnotize, and nothing advances your confidence in your ability to hypnotize more than having success with your early experiences in hypnotizing.

Fred Roggin (Roggin's Heroes), NBC Channel 4, Los Angeles, challenges Tom Silver into hypnotizing viewers and having them do fun things on live television sports show, "Sunday Night Sports". 1999

CHAPTER SEVEN

FURTHER PRELIMINARY HYPNOTIC KNOWLEDGE YOU SHOULD HAVE

WHAT IS HYPNOSIS?

Perhaps the simplest way to answer this question is to say that hypnosis is a state of mind produced through the use of suggestions, amplified by the energy of the hypnotist causing a mental condition of hypersuggestibility.

Outwardly hypnosis appears much like a state of sleep. However, internally it is quite different. In normal sleep, the attention of the sleeper is diffused, while in hypnotic sleep the attention of the sleeper is concentrated towards the suggestions presented by the hypnotist. A person may be awake and still be hypnotized. It may also by self-induced. What is of special interest is that the power of suggestion is both used to induce the state and to control the state it induces.

To understand hypnosis, it must be understood that mind functions on two levels: one, our normal waking state which we call conscious mind, and two, on an inner level which we call subconscious mind. Hypnosis brings into action the subconscious phase of mind in which the subject (often called the "hypnotic") responds spontaneously and uncritically to the suggestions of the hypnotist. While in that state, the "hypnotic" is not capable of inductive reasoning and cannot analyze, so to speak, what is real from the unreal.

You will find there is a considerable difference in the actions of different people being hypnotically influenced.

Some become entranced quickly (falling into a sleep-like state), and have no memory of the experience (or what occurred while in it) on being aroused. Some at first respond only to waking hypnosis tests. Others will on a first or second trial go into a light trance without complete amnesia. The memory recall is of a hazy nature, much like recalling an almost forgotten dream. As the induction is repeated several times, often the subject will drop down to deeper levels.

Once hypnosis has been induced in a subject who has amnesia on awakening from trance, he can be quickly returned to profound hypnosis by looking him straight in the eye and saying in a positive voice, "SLEEP!" and he will instantly reenter hypnosis.

Generally speaking, there are four major stages in hypnosis:

1ST DEGREE

In this state, a person is influenced in the waking state without any attempt to induce trance (hypnotic sleep). He knows what he is doing but is unable to resist the operator's suggestions.

2ND DEGREE

In this state, a light sleep, drowsiness, or reverie is induced, and the subject will accept suggestions from the operator which will cause mental aberrations and bodily sensations.

3RD DEGREE

In this state, we find somnambulism. In it, catalepsy and anesthesia may be produced, and hallucinations caused to appear. In this state, post-hypnotic phenomena may be developed (hypnotic occurrences happening following the termination of the trance). On awakening from this state there is amnesia as to what occurred during the trance.

4TH DEGREE

In this advanced state of hypnosis, the psychic powers of the mind seem to advance. Clairvoyance can be produced and telepathy manifested. It is the ESP realm of the mind. Only a relatively small percentage of people seem to show these special abilities. If a subject has talent in this direction, it is well to concentrate hypnotic work with them along psychic lines.

Even subjects in profound hypnosis will be found different in their individual reactions to the suggestions given. Some in deep trance become lethargic, while others respond with vigor.

You will find some people who say they are willing to be hypnotized will offer unconscious resistance to being influenced. Some even resist being influenced in simple tests. But on trying such a subject a second time on the following day, frequently hypnosis will ensue. In your initial practice of hypnotism, never give up. Persevere. You will even amaze yourself with the results that will come your way.

DIFFERENT METHODS OF HYPNOTIZING

All people are not affected by the same method of being hypnotized. People differ in their responses. While one person will respond best to an authoritarian (father) approach, another will respond to a gentle (mother) approach. The art of becoming an expert hypnotist comes in learning which hypnotic method will best influence the specific subject being worked with. It is an art that comes only through experience. It is almost an intuition as to what is best to do. Here is a generalized list of the most popular methods of hypnotizing:

1. By verbalized suggestions (oral techniques).
2. By mental suggestions (mesmeric techniques).
3. By fixation of the gaze upon a bright object (Braid techniques).
4. By fascination.
5. By contact passes with the subject.
6. By noncontact passes over the subject.
7. By monotonous procedures.
8. By loud and unexpected noises.
9. By the lulling effect of soft music (lullaby techniques).
10. By the use of mechanical devices such as revolving spirals and flashing lights.
11. By a combination of mesmeric and suggestion techniques.
12. By autosuggestion to one's self (self-hypnosis).

There are countless variations of these methods, but these procedures are the basics.

THE AROUSING (AWAKENING) FROM HYPNOSIS

Usually hypnosis may be terminated simply by the direct suggestion to "Wake Up". Be gentle in arousing the subject, just as you would personally like to awaken from deep sleep.

Another method is to blow on the eyes two or three times. A sprinkle of water on the face will have the same effect. Occasionally the subject will enjoy the state of hypnosis so much that they wish to remain in the trance. If so, just let them sleep and they will arouse themselves when ready. The influence will invariably wear off and natural sleep will result.

The mind likes to do things in steps so a popular method of awakening subjects from hypnosis is to suggest:

> *"I will count slowly from one to five, and at the count of FIVE you will be wide awake and feeling fine."*

Then count. The subject awakens.

In awakening the subject when hypnosis is used for therapeutic purposes, the subject can be told to awaken when he has benefited from the healing suggestions presented.

CHAPTER EIGHT

THREE PRELIMINARY TESTS IN WAKING HYPNOSIS

Now that you have background knowledge for understanding hypnotism and the laws of its operation, instructions for developing your hypnotic eyes and voice combined with methods to present suggestions that influence, you are ready to perform some preliminary test demonstrations in hypnotism. It is the method of experimenting with experiencing. In other words, the most effective way to learn hypnotism is by hypnotizing.

If you were to study mathematics, you would start with arithmetic before you advance to calculus. It is the same with mastering hypnotism. Start with the less complex and advance to the more complex.

There are three good preliminary tests following with which you can begin your practice.

Waking hypnosis experiments are good to begin with, for while the basic subconscious phenomena is the same, we are more familiar with our waking state than we are with our sleeping state of mind.

In this HOW-TO BOOK OF HYPNOTISM, you are instructed in exactly how to present each experiment, inclusive of the detailed word-for-word formula of suggestions to be used to successfully accomplish each test. Nothing is left to guesswork for you; do exactly as you are instructed and you will accomplish amazing things.

To successfully accomplish these experiments, at all times use this threefold formula of visualization, affirmation and projection. That is:

1. VISUALIZATION
   Form within your mind a mental picture of exactly how the subject is going to respond in being hypnotized for the performance of the test. See it happening.

2. AFFIRMATION
   Verbalize, in a positive manner, the suggestions that cause the subjective mind of the subject to perform exactly as you have visualized. Tell it as you see it.

3. PROJECTION
   See in your "mind's eye" the hypnotic response you have visualized and affirmed as being projected into the subconscious mind of the subject, automatically causing the hypnotic effect to be accomplished. Project it as you tell it.

Perform these experiments with a willing subject in the order given: 1 -2 - 3. Understand! You are set! You are ready! READY, SET, GO ...

EXPERIMENT ONE
CAUSING A SUBJECT TO FALL BACKWARD

Have him stand up, facing towards a wall, and tell him to place his feet together[1]. Arms should be at the sides of his body. Have him hold his arms at his sides with hands open fully. Ask him to relax his entire body. That is, he should stand naturally upright sensing within himself that the

---

[1] You can perform all hypnotic experiments with either sex. In these instructions, the masculine gender is used for literary convenience. - Ed.

muscles of his body are free from all stiffness - they are relaxed. By standing behind him and pulling him back with your hand on his shoulder, you can tell if he has done as requested. If he comes back easily, he has obeyed you; if he resists, he has not followed your instructions and done as you requested. In such a case, explain that for this experiment in waking hypnosis to successfully operate for him, it is essential that he relax his muscles as he stands erect.

Having obtained the right conditions in him, say:

> "Now, THINK that your body is going to start swaying backward -- that you are going to fall over backwards. Think of nothing else. You will soon feel as if something compelled you to fall back, but do not be afraid. I am standing right behind you, and as you fall I will catch you. When you feel the impulse to fall do not resist it, but just let yourself go."

Then have him hold up his head and tell him to close his eyes. Now, stand directly back of the subject. Stand at a distance of about three feet behind him, just so far that your hands reach easily to the temples of his head from behind ... tip his head back slightly towards yourself so your fingertips rest on the crown of his head, base of the brain (nap of the neck). Then continue on moving your hands down the spine to the hips, on to the very end of the spine. This is called a "contact pass". It should be made lightly, using just enough pressure so as not to distract the equilibrium of the subject. Make three of these contact passes down the spine.

Then return both hands and place them at the temples on each side of the head and verbally suggest:

> "When .. I .. withdraw .. my .. hands .. from .. you, you .. will .. slowly .. fall .. backwards."

Repeat these suggestions until he topples over backwards into your waiting arms. Catch him safely and immediately return him to his feet.

Be sure during all of this process to concentrate your mind on the one idea that he will fall backwards. Use your willpower. The more firmly you believe that you can draw him backwards, the quicker the results will be obtained.

As you learn how to perform this experiment, study every step in sequence so you know exactly what to say and do in 1-2-3 order. Learn this lesson well, the movement and the words, so you can perform it in complete confidence that it will unfailingly operate. Be sure to withdraw your fingers slowly from the back of his head and present your suggestions of his falling slowly and positively. It is important to learn how to perform this test perfectly as it sets the pattern of effectively influencing subjects in the waking state that you will use in the many forms of waking hypnosis you will learn how to do.

If the subject should feel a little dazed after falling backwards, snap your fingers close to his ear and say, *"All right ... you are just fine"*.

When you have successfully performed this first test, you are ready to perform the second.

EXPERIMENT TWO
CAUSING A SUBJECT TO FALL FORWARD

In this experiment you cause the subject to fall forwards, exactly opposite to the first test. The handling is very similar to your handling of the first test, except in this instance you use the eyes.

Have the subject stand facing you. His eyes should be in the shadow while facing you and your eyes in the light while facing him. Tell him to relax his muscles and look you straight in the eyes.

Ask him to think of nothing but falling forward. Look him squarely in the eyes, concentrating your gaze at the root of his nose -- at the central point between his eyes. Keep a sober, earnest demeanor and have the subject do the same. Say to him:

> "Look .. at .. me .. Concentrate .. your .. attention .. fully .. upon .. my .. eyes."

Speak positively to him. Command him. Tell him exactly what you want him to do.

Then place your hands at the temples of his face, one on each side. Look at him steadily in the eyes for some 15 seconds while holding the thought in your mind of his falling towards you. Then say slowly:

> "When I .. remove .. my .. hands .. from .. you, .. you .. will .. slowly .. fall .. forward."

As you give these suggestions, withdraw your hands away slowly forward on his temples. Let your movements be subtle and gentle and keep on saying:

> "You .. are .. falling ... falling ... falling .. forward. You .. cannot .. stop .. falling. Have .. no .. fear. I .. will .. catch .. you .. when .. you .. fall."

Repeat these suggestions over and over until he falls forward into your arms. The repetition of suggestions has a compounding effect in developing power. Draw your own body slightly downwards while withdrawing your hands. Catch him firmly when he falls.

Properly performed, your success with this experiment in waking hypnosis will be excellent.

EXPERIMENT THREE
STIFFENING A SUBJECT'S ARM

Having successfully performed the two preceding experiments in waking hypnosis, you are ready for this one. In this preliminary test, you use a combination process of eyes, suggestion and passes.

Hypnotic passes are made in a downward direction with palms turned inwards toward the subject; that is from any given point downward towards the feet, never upwards towards the head. All upward passes dispel the influence. All downward passes lead toward hypnosis.

There are contact passes and noncontact passes. Contact passes are made downward with a light stroking motion upon the body. A contact pass is just as effective on top of the clothing as upon the bare skin. A contact pass is usually made on individual parts of the body, such as on an arm, leg, head, etc..

Noncontact passes are made downward with the hands held about two inches above the surface of the body and end their sweep at the end of the spine or at the feet. Noncontact passes are mostly used to induce trance states. In making passes, the fingers should be slightly spread apart and the passes made slowly. Each method of passes should be used where it belongs. If the former is used, contact should be from start to finish. If the latter, care should be used not to touch the subject at all. Passes carry suggestions in themselves combined with a transference of bodily energy from hypnotist to subject.

The physical effect of passes will be noticed by subjects in different ways. Some will experience numbness coming into the body over which passes are made. Others seem to sense an electric-like tingling in the skin. Still others report sensations of heat and coldness. Whenever you make use of passes, it is essential that you direct your will to the effect you wish to produce.

You are now ready to perform this third experiment of stiffening the subject's arm.

Have the subject stand before you and take hold of his right arm. Pull out the arm straight from his shoulder and tell him to make a fist and to stiffen his entire arm. Your left hand now grasps the closed fist; hold it up on a level with his shoulder.

Now look him straight in the eyes or between them at the root of the nose. With your right hand, you commence to make contact passes from the shoulder of the arm held out to the hand. Make three such passes with a light, stroking motion. While you are making the passes, say to the subject:

> "Think .. that .. your .. arm .. is .. stiff .. and .. that .. you ..
> cannot .. bend it. Look .. at .. me .. squarely .. in .. the ..
> eyes .. and .. do .. not .. blink. When .. I .. count .. three, ..
> you .. will .. find .. your .. arm .. has .. become .. so .. stiff ..
> and .. rigid .. that .. you .. cannot .. bend it .. no .. matter ..
> how .. hard .. you .. try. It .. has .. become .. rigid .. like .. a
> .. bar .. of steel .. and .. the .. more .. you .. try .. to .. bend ..
> it, .. the .. stiffer .. it .. will .. become. Now then, .. when .. I
> .. count .. three, .. you .. cannot .. bend .. your .. arm .. no ..
> matter .. how .. hard .. you .. try. One .. two .. THREE! ..
> Try ... try hard ... your arm .. is .. stiff, .. stiffer, ... stiff.
> You .. cannot .. bend .. it. Try. ... Try hard! .. You .. cannot
> .. bend .. your .. arm."

After the subject has tried to bend his arm and found he cannot do so, say to him:

> "All right now, the influence has flowed away and you can
> bend your arm. The hypnotic influence is gone!"

In performing this test, speak positively and in a commanding tone. Count in a rising tone: *"One, two,* and emphasize *"THREE!"* as a positive command. At the moment you say "three", point your right forefinger at him in a forceful manner which serves to drive home the suggestions.

Tom Silver performing the famous hand locking test and setting world record for hypnotizing the most people (3,800) at the same time through an interpreter. Taipei Athletic Stadium, Taipei, Taiwan, R.O.C.. February 1995

CHAPTER NINE

THE FAMOUS HAND LOCKING TEST

Having successfully performed the three foregoing preliminary waking hypnosis experiments, you are ready for the fourth. The Hand Locking Test was made famous by the French psychologist, Emile Coue, who demonstrated it in all his lectures and used it as a method to test his client's responsiveness to autosuggestion in his clinic.

For this test, have the subject stand in front of you and concentrate upon your eyes. Ask him to put his hands together with palms clasped and fingers interlocked. Have him straighten out both arms and make them stiff. Then suggest:

> *"Squeeze .. your .. hands .. tightly .. together .. and .. think .. that .. you .. cannot .. pull .. them .. apart. They .. have .. become .. locked .. so .. tightly .. together .. that .. you .. cannot .. pull .. them .. apart .. no .. matter .. how .. hard .. you .. try. Try hard. .. Your .. hands .. are .. locked .. so .. tightly .. together .. you .. cannot .. pull .. them .. apart .. no .. matter .. how .. hard .. you .. try. .. Pull ... pull. Try .. try .. try. You .. cannot .. unlock .. your .. hands .. with .. all .. your .. might. Your .. hands .. are .. locked .. together. You .. cannot .. get .. your .. hands .. apart."*

If your subject has been following your suggestions with earnest concentration, his hands will have become so firmly locked together that struggle as he will he simply cannot pull his locked hands apart.

After the subject has tried in vain to release his hands, snap your fingers beside his ear and state:

47

"All .. right .. now, .. the .. influence .. is .. all .. gone .. now. Relax. You .. can .. take .. your .. hands .. apart .. now."

In presenting suggestions to subjects in performing waking hypnosis experiments, speak positively, slowly and distinctly, becoming more and more forceful as the test proceeds towards its climax.

Throw your energy into the performance of these tests. Having succeeded with these four experiments, you will gain confidence in your ability to hypnotically influence people. Mastering the art of how to present suggestions that influence will put new life into your whole personality. All tests of this muscular nature in waking hypnosis follow this pattern.

CHAPTER TEN

FURTHER EXPERIMENTS IN WAKING HYPNOSIS YOU CAN PERFORM

CAUSING A STIFF LEG

Have the subject put his whole weight on his right leg, which should be put forward as if to march. Make it stiff. Tell him to think he cannot bend it. Take his right hand in yours and have him concentrate his attention upon your eyes. Tell him to follow your eyes at all times, as you suggest:

> "Follow .. my .. eyes .. as .. I .. bend .. down .. and .. make .. your .. leg .. become .. stiff .. so .. you .. cannot .. bend .. it."

Keep his eyes fixed on yours as you bend down and make a few passes down his leg with your hands commencing about six inches above the knee and press slightly on the knee joint. While making these contact passes, continue to suggest:

> "Now .. you .. will .. find .. your .. leg .. becoming .. stiff, .. stiffer, .. stiffer ... stiff .. and .. you .. cannot .. bend it .. no .. matter .. how .. hard .. you .. try. The knee .. joint .. is .. getting .. so .. stiff .. you .. cannot .. bend .. it. It .. is .. impossible .. to .. bend .. your .. leg. It .. is .. stiff .. stiff .. stiff. It .. is .. impossible .. for .. you .. to .. bend .. your .. leg .. as .. it .. is .. stiff .. stiff .. stiff! Try .. to .. bend .. it. You .. cannot .. do .. it. Try ... try hard."

As you say these last suggestions, slowly rise up, still retaining his gaze fixed on your eyes, and pull him towards you actually causing him to walk stiff-legged.

Make him walk. He will walk stiff-legged. After he has walked a dozen or so feet on his stiff leg, remove the influence by striking your hands together as you say:

> *"All right .. it .. is .. all .. gone .. now. You .. are .. free. You .. can .. bend .. your .. leg .. now."*

CANNOT SIT DOWN

To prevent a person from sitting down, have him stand in front of a chair. Stiffen both his legs by the method just described, except that the subject should have both feet together. Then tell him he cannot sit at your count of three. Count THREE and point your fingers at him. Release him by the same process described.

CANNOT GET UP

Have subject sit in a chair with his hands on his thighs and his feet flat on the floor. Now look him in the eyes or at the root of his nose, and ask him to imagine he cannot get up. Keep your eyes steadily on him and say:

> *"When .. I .. count .. three .. you .. will .. find .. that .. you .. cannot .. get .. up .. from .. the .. chair. The more .. you .. try .. to .. get .. up .. the .. more .. impossible .. it .. becomes. You .. are .. glued .. to .. the .. chair. One .. two .. THREE! Try .. it. It .. is .. impossible .. for .. you .. to .. get .. up. .. Try .. hard .. as .. you .. will."*

After he has made frantic efforts to get up, snap your fingers and say:

> "All .. right! Now .. you .. can .. get .. up."

MAKING THE SUBJECT FOLLOW YOU

Stand in front of the subject. Hold your forefinger, of either hand, about four inches in front of his eyes and say to him:

> "Look .. at .. my .. finger... Concentrate .. on .. my .. finger .. and .. when .. I .. count .. three .. you .. will .. follow .. my .. finger .. wherever .. it .. goes. You .. cannot .. look .. away. Follow .. my .. finger."

Now walk away in any direction you please and he will obediently follow your finger. Release by usual method.

CANNOT JUMP OVER STICK

Lay a stick on the floor in front of subject and tell him to think he cannot jump over it. Look fixedly at the root of his nose. Then stiffen his legs as has been described and say to him he cannot jump over the stick when you count three. Point your finger at him and say positively:

> "You .. cannot .. do .. it! Try .. it .. and .. see."

End test by usual method.

51

CANNOT SPEAK HIS NAME

Stand in front of subject. Look him in the eyes for about ten seconds. Place your right hand around his throat and ask him to think he cannot speak his name. Keep your gaze fixed. Then say:

> *"When .. I .. count .. three .. you .. will .. be .. unable .. to .. say .. your .. own .. name. You .. are .. tongue-tied. It .. is .. impossible .. for .. you .. to .. say .. your .. own .. name. One .. two .. THREE! You .. cannot .. say .. it!"*

Some subjects will move their jaws without uttering a sound; others will make frantic efforts to try to speak. End the experiment in the usual way.

CANNOT OPEN HIS EYES

Have subject take a seat and look into his eyes for ten or fifteen seconds. Then ask him to close his eyes. When he does this, make one or two contact passes with your thumbs over the eyelids pressing in lightly, starting from the sides of the eyes towards the nose, and say to him:

> *"When .. I .. count .. three .. your .. eyelids .. will .. be .. stuck .. so .. tightly .. together .. that .. you .. cannot .. open .. them. The .. more .. you .. try .. to .. open .. them .. the .. tighter .. they .. will .. stick. (Repeat) One .. two .. THREE! You .. cannot .. open .. your .. eyes .. Try .. as .. hard .. as .. you .. will."*

Performed well, invariably the subject will be unable to open his eyes. In some cases even the eyelids will not move.

No amount of struggling makes it possible for him to open his eyes. It is an effective test.

There is a knack to properly giving suggestions that makes them register as a subconscious response. It is a gift for the hypnotist and a skill that comes with practice. Practice. Practice. Practice. You will have excellent success.

SUGGESTIONS FOR DIFFERENT TESTS

There are all manner of effective experiments you can perform with waking hypnosis, such as these:

Cannot drop broom.
Cannot pick up stick.
Cannot close mouth.
Cannot remember name.
Cannot walk backward.
Cannot raise hands from lap.
Cannot shut hands.
Cannot drop arm, etc., etc., etc..

Use your creative imagination and you will come up with numerous effective tests you can perform with waking hypnosis. Just adhere to these general rules when you perform such feats:

1. Have subject look you in the eyes without blinking.
2. Tell subject to think of what you want him to think.
3. Let your suggestions clearly express the effects you wish to obtain in the subject.
4. Formulate your suggestions precisely like a command.
5. Give your suggestions positively like a command.
6. Often present a cue/time for the suggestion to go

into effect such as the count of, "One .. two .. three".

7. Emphasize the "THREE" as the time when the effect is to occur and reinforce the effect by a direct finger pointing at the subject.

8. End each test with a snap of the fingers or clap of the hands near ear of subject, combined with the suggestion, "All .. right .. the .. influence .. is .. gone .. now .. and .. you .. feel .. just .. fine."

In working with new subjects, it is well advised to repeat the suggestions to drive them home into the subconscious. Repetition is the driving force of suggestion. When a subject has been previously hypnotized, it is only necessary to look him in the eyes and present one time the desired suggestion and it will occur.

Apply these rules and you will find the effects of waking hypnosis amazing.

CHAPTER ELEVEN

INFLUENCING A NUMBER OF PEOPLE AT THE SAME TIME WITH WAKING HYPNOSIS

THE ROTATING HANDS

Select a number of subjects with whom you have been successful in performing the foregoing tests. Seat them in a semicircle in straight chairs without arms. Stand about five feet in front of the group. Look from one to another slowly and tell them to look into your eyes. Then look straight ahead and it will seem to each one as though you are looking directly at him or her individually. Now say to them:

> "Take .. your .. hands .. and .. revolve .. them .. around .. one .. another. Make .. them .. go .. faster .. faster .. faster. Look .. at .. me."

As you give these instructions, start revolving your own hands around and around each other, faster and faster as you continue with your suggestions:

> "Revolve .. your .. hands .. around .. and .. around .. each .. other .. faster .. and .. faster, .. and .. when .. I .. count .. three .. you .. will .. find .. that .. you .. cannot .. stop .. revolving .. your .. hands .. around .. each .. other, .. and .. the .. more .. you .. try .. to .. stop .. the .. faster .. you .. will .. make .. them .. go. One .. two .. three. You .. cannot .. stop .. try .. hard .. as .. you .. will. Try .. it! Try .. it!."

After the group have revolved their hands swiftly around and around each other, go to each subject separately, clap your hands next to his ear and say:

"All .. right. You .. can .. stop .. now. Relax .. and .. rest .. your .. hands .. on .. your .. lap."

In performing these experiments and all other group tests, always commence by having the subjects sit upright in their chairs with feet flat on the floor and hands resting on their laps. Both feet and arms should be kept separate; never allow them to be crossed.

THE SLAPPING THIGHS / THE SHAKING HANDS

In the same manner, you can cause the group to continue slapping their thighs or wave their hands wildly in the air.

THE MISSING FINGERTIPS

Another group experiment that is effective in waking hypnosis is to tell the subjects to hold up their hands, palms towards the chest, bending all fingers inwards except the index finger of each hand. Ask them to touch the fingertips of the two index fingers. When they do so, have them move these fingertips about four inches apart and keep the hands in that position. Now suggest:

"Look .. at .. me .. right .. in .. the .. eyes .. and .. when .. I .. count .. three .. you .. will .. find .. that .. you .. cannot .. make .. your .. fingertips .. meet .. no .. matter .. how .. hard .. you .. try. The .. more .. you .. try .. to .. touch .. them .. together .. the .. more .. they .. will .. miss. Try, ..

56

try .. hard. The .. more .. you .. try .. the .. more .. they .. will .. miss."

The subjects will try in every conceivable manner to make their fingers meet, without success. To conclude the test, say:

"All ... right .. stop .. trying .. now. The .. test .. is .. over. Rest .. your .. hands .. in .. your .. lap."

Group tests in waking hypnosis are very amusing to an audience. Practice performing these waking hypnosis tests as much as possible. They will provide you with the skill of using the power of suggestion in your daily communication with people. They give you a magnetic personality.

The ambitious person attains success most often by climbing the ladder one rung at a time. That is why it is advisable that you master each step perfectly so you know the steps like your A-B-C's before attempting the greater and more complicated experiments which follow later on as you advance into the field of hypnotherapy. A good hypnotist can accomplish many wonderful things. Cures can be obtained where medicine has failed, pain can be relieved, mental worries and stress reduced by hypnotic influence. In functional disorders such as insomnia, drinking, tobacco and drug habits, it is often the very best remedy. In some cases, it has been used very successfully as an anesthetic.

You are now ready to advance to learning how to induce the hypnotic sleep.

CHAPTER TWELVE

HOW TO INDUCE HYPNOTIC SLEEP

Hypnotic sleep is the trance state of hypnosis. It is the state that many people regard as really being hypnotized. Outwardly the subject in this state appears to be sleeping, although in reality the inner mind activity is the reverse. In normal sleep the attention is diffused, while in the hypnotic sleep it is very concentrated upon the point and/or objective as directed by the hypnotist. The hypnotic sleep takes you to deeper levels of hypnosis and is characterized by hyper-suggestibility. It has been said that the effect of suggestions given in the trance state versus the waking state could be compared to a rifle versus a shotgun. In the trance depths of hypnosis, they go right on target.

Before attempting to put a subject into hypnotic sleep, first become master of waking hypnosis. Then you are ready.

Putting the subject asleep in hypnosis calls for smooth handling. Know exactly what you are doing. Show confidence in every action. Confidence begets confidence.

In this text, you will be shown a variety of methods to produce hypnotic sleep, commencing with an effective method that will hypnotize the majority of subjects. It is a methodical method and a good one to practice as you learn hypnotic techniques.

As much as possible, conduct your first experiments in putting subjects to sleep in a quiet place. Use a private room free of disturbances. Explain to the subject that the experience will make him relaxed and sleepy, and will be much like drifting off into a pleasant nap. Always get the consent of the subject in inducing hypnotic states. You are ready ...

Seat the subject in a chair, preferably a straight back chair. Any light entering the room should come from behind the subject and be directed on you. Have him place his feet flat on the floor and rest his hands on his thighs. Tell him to make himself comfortable and to relax his muscles. Then take a pencil or other object; it makes no difference. To make this lesson clearer, we will use a pencil with a shiny tip. Stand in front of the seated person on his right side. Now hold the pencil about five inches from his eyes high enough so that he will have to open them wide and look forward to the shiny tip of the pencil. It should be held in between his eyes so that the pupils of his eyes will converge as much as possible as he stares at the tip of the pencil held before him. In a sense, he looks cross-eyed. You will get the point if you look at the tip of your nose. It fatigues the eyes rapidly.

Tell him to look with both eyes at the shiny tip of the pencil. Tell him to concentrate his vision upon that tip and to look at nothing else until his eyes get so tired he cannot keep them open any longer. Hold the pencil still and at the same time direct your own gaze at the root of his nose and concentrate your mind on the idea that he will go to sleep. Tell him to think of going to sleep but not to close his eyes until he simply cannot keep them open any longer. Soon his eyes will start to blink and water as he stares. Soon he will close them. You can facilitate the closing of the eyes by giving the following suggestions as soon as you notice him blinking:

> "Your .. eyelids .. are .. getting .. heavy. .. They .. commence .. to .. blink. You .. cannot .. keep .. them .. open .. any .. longer. Your .. eyes .. are .. watering. They .. are .. tired, .. they .. feel .. heavy, .. they .. are .. closing .. now .. and .. you .. are .. becoming .. sleepy. Very .. very .. sleepy. When .. I .. count .. to .. ten, .. your .. eyes .. will .. close .. and .. you .. will .. be .. asleep, .. fast .. asleep."

Count slowly from one to ten in a low, even tone. In many cases, the subject's eyes will be closed by the time you have counted to ten but if they are not, gently close them by passing your hand over them. As soon as the eyes close, place your left hand on top of his head and make passes with your right hand across his forehead from the left temple to the right temple and give these suggestions:

"You .. are .. so .. sleepy. Sleepy .. drowsy .. sleepy .. drowsy .. soooo .. sleepy. So .. very .. very .. sleepy. Your .. head .. feels .. heavy .. soooo .. sleepy ... soooo .. tired. You .. cannot .. keep .. awake .. any .. longer .. you .. are .. so .. sleepy. You .. hear .. nothing .. but .. the .. drone .. of .. my .. voice. You .. are .. going .. sound .. asleep .. fast .. asleep .. sound .. asleep. Your .. head .. feels .. heavy .. like .. lead. You .. cannot .. hold .. it .. up .. any .. longer, .. it's .. falling .. down .. upon .. your chest. You .. are .. going .. fast .. to .. sleep. Sleep, .. sleep, .. sleep. You .. are .. fast .. asleep, .. sound .. asleep. .. Everything .. is .. dark .. before .. you. You .. cannot .. move .. your .. arms .. because .. they .. are .. so .. heavy .. and .. you .. cannot .. move .. your .. legs .. because .. they .. are .. so .. heavy .. too. Your .. whole .. body .. feels .. numb. You .. hear .. nothing .. but .. my .. voice. When .. I .. count .. ten .. you .. will .. be .. fast .. asleep. One .. two .. three .. four .. five .. six .. seven .. eight .. nine .. TEN. You are fast asleep. FAST .. ASLEEP!"

Say the last "FAST .. ASLEEP" in a commanding tone. After you have made passes across his forehead while giving these suggestions, then change your position and stand directly in front of him. Now make downward sweeping passes over his body from the top of the head towards his feet with both your hands (all the while continuing to suggest the "sleep formula"). Keep your gaze centered on the subject's forehead between the closed eyes while speaking and making passes. Spread your fingers slightly and use both hands as mentioned. Do not touch subject's body in making the passes; make them at least an inch above the surface of the body. Make the passes very slowly and when you get to the knees, turn palms outward (away from the body) and bring them with an upward motion to the top of the head again. In doing this, spread your arms so as to make a half circle on each side of his body from the knees to the head and then start the downward passes again.

Use this pass for about five minutes in silence and then softly give the "sleep formula" again. As you do this, lay the palm of your hands over his eyes when making the suggestion that everything is dark before his eyes. As soon as his head drops, you will find that hypnotic sleep has been produced. Now insist that he cannot waken until you tell him to and emphasize the fact that he cannot hear anything but your voice.

THE TEST OF HYPNOTIC SLEEP

This provides a good test that the subject is in hypnotic trance. When you think he is sleeping soundly, lift up his right or left arm to a horizontal position and say to him:

"Your .. arm .. is .. suspended .. up .. and .. you .. cannot .. drop .. it .. try .. as .. hard .. as .. you .. will. Try .. try .. hard! You .. cannot .. move .. it .. at .. all."

If it remains up against his efforts to lower it, you have a good indication that he is hypnotized.

This arm stiffening test for hypnotic sleep can also be used to deepen the trance state. Suggest:

61

*"You .. cannot .. move .. your .. arm .. because .. it .. is .. so
.. stiff .. but .. you .. will .. find .. it .. begins .. to .. feel .. so
.. tired .. it .. is .. commencing .. to .. slowly .. drop .. down
.. to .. your .. lap .. and .. as .. it .. drops .. down .. you ..
will .. go .. deeper .. and .. deeper .. asleep .. in .. hypnosis ..
and .. when .. it .. finally .. reaches .. your .. lap .. you ..
will .. be .. deeply .. asleep .. in .. profound .. hypnosis.
You .. will .. be .. profoundly .. hypnotized."*

While in hypnotic sleep, the subject will perform a variety of suggestions you present. Hypnotic sleep produces a mental state of mind that is hypersuggestible. The hypnotized subject will carry out the suggestions as true to his nature. If he is slow in his natural state, he will react slowly while in hypnosis. If he is lively and quick-witted, he will act correspondingly when hypnotized. In this state, you can present your suggestions in a forceful, commanding manner. Most important is that they be readily understood. Here is an effective experiment you can use to further test the hypnotic responsiveness of the subject:

Place your left hand on top of subject's head with your thumb resting at the root of his nose. Then say:

*"It .. is .. beginning .. to .. get .. very .. warm .. in .. this ..
room. It .. is .. getting .. so .. warm .. you .. are ..
beginning .. to .. perspire. You .. want .. to .. fan ..
yourself .. to .. cool .. off. It .. is .. becoming .. positively..
hot! Take .. off .. your .. jacket .. and .. get .. cool. Ah ..
that .. is .. better .. now .. and .. you .. are .. becoming ..
comfortable. The .. temperature .. is .. going .. down ..
now, .. and .. you .. are .. sleeping .. comfortably .. in ..
your .. chair. Go .. even .. more .. deeply .. asleep .. in ..
hypnosis .. now."*

In response to these suggestions, the subject will begin to perspire, will fan himself, and take off his coat. He will then

62

drop down more deeply asleep in hypnosis, exactly as you have told him. There are almost no limits (providing such are not in opposition to the subject's inner moral nature) to the variety of things you can have the hypnotized subject respond to.

Hypnosis is a subconscious mind phenomena. The subconscious accepts, without hesitation or doubt, every statement that is made to it no matter how absurd, incongruous, or contrary to the objective experience of the individual. The subconscious never classifies a series of known facts and reasons from them up to general principles, but given a general principle to start with, it will reason deductively from that down to all legitimate inferences with a marvelous cogency and power. The subject takes the text from the hypnotist, but he may amplify and develop it enormously of his own creation as he acts it out.

The subject may be rendered happy and laughing, or sad and dejected, angry or pleased, liberal or stingy, proud or vain, pugnacious or pacific, bold or timid, hopeful or despondent, insolent or respectful. He may be made to sing, shout, weep, act, dance, shoot, fish, preach, pray, deliver an eloquent oration or expound a profound argument.

The expression during these responses to suggestions is also important. In all such experiments, it will be observed that the gestures and voice, the manner and expression, the whole physiognomy and natural language are extremely perfect. The attitude of pride, humility, anger, fear, kindness, pugnacity, devotion or mediation and all others are, with individuality of expression in each case, in accordance to his personality.

The attitudes and gestures are equal or surpassing the best efforts of an accomplished actor, although the subject normally shows no acting ability in the waking state. Everyone knows how difficult it is to place oneself in a particular position so that the expression, the attitude, and the actions should correspond to the idea. To represent such a situation as naturally as possible is the art of the seasoned actor; but it is seldom realized on the stage. And it is still more difficult to change the mind in a moment and pass from one situation to another in a few seconds. The hypnotized subject, however, does so easily.

POSTHYPNOSIS

One of the most important phenomena is posthypnotic suggestions. These are deferred suggestions given to the subject during hypnosis which take effect after waking. The subject, while in trance, is given a suggestion which he is told he will perform after he is aroused from the trance. The deeper the hypnosis, the greater will be the success of posthypnotic suggestions. When he is recalled to his waking state, he has no recollection of having received any instructions, but at the time stated or when the circumstances arise, he will proceed to do what has been suggested to him while he was hypnotized. The suggestion is carried out by the subject usually accepting such as being his own motivation for performing the acting.

All phenomena which can be hypnotically produced while the subject is in hypnosis can equally occur as posthypnotic experience. Posthypnotic suggestions are invariably used in all forms of hypnotherapy in which the client is given suggestions that carry over into his daily life for personal benefit.

It is marvelous that this is so, otherwise the use of suggestive therapeutics would be extremely limited. That is to say, if suggestions only had influence over a person while in trance, their therapy value would be limited. It is through posthypnosis that the value of hypnotic suggestions carry over to aid in the daily art of living.

HOW TO AWAKEN THE SUBJECT FROM THE HYPNOTIC SLEEP

Since hypnosis is induced by a process of suggestion affirming ideas of going to sleep, it stands to reason that reversing the process by presenting suggestions for the removal of sleep and awakening from the trance is bound to remove the hypnotic condition, i.e. awaken and/or arouse the hypnotized person.

The arousal from hypnosis should always be a gentle process, just as you would want if someone were to awaken you from a deep sleep. Just keep in mind that in inducing the hypnotic condition, you presented your suggestions slowly and with care so apply this same gentle, calm approach to the removal of the hypnotic sleep. Remember also, as a hypnotist it is your obligation to always arouse the subject feeling fine and well in every way.

Having caused all the suggestions of your hypnotic experiments to fade away from the mind of the subject and suggesting that he is sleeping peacefully, present these suggestions:

> "All .. right, I'm .. going .. to .. count .. from .. one .. to .. FIVE. When .. I .. reach .. the .. count .. of .. FIVE .. you .. will .. be ..wide .. awake. I'm .. starting .. to .. count .. so .. get .. ready .. to .. awaken .. now. One .. Two .. You .. are .. beginning .. to .. wake .. up. Three .. Your .. eyes .. are .. opening, you .. want .. to .. move .. about .. and .. stretch .. Four .. You .. are .. waking .. up. FIVE. Wake-up. You .. are .. wide .. awake .. and .. are .. feeling .. fine!"

Under the influence of these suggestions, your subject will gradually open his eyes, move about, stretch himself and awaken feeling fine.

Occasionally, you may run into a subject who enjoys being in hypnosis so much he is loath to arouse from hypnosis on the moment. That is of no concern. Just allow an opportunity for some more moments for the hypnosis to be enjoyed. Left entirely to himself, the subject will soon pass from the hypnotic sleep into natural sleep and will awaken on his own accord exactly as he does on arising each morning following a refreshing night's sleep.

Country Music's "Female Artist of the Year," Martina McBride, watches as "The Amazing Tom Silver" puts radio station listener into a trance and transforms him into country music singer, Clint Black. Radio Station KMEL, Phoenix, Arizona. 1997

CHAPTER THIRTEEN

OTHER METHODS OF INDUCING HYPNOTIC SLEEP

The method of inducing hypnotic sleep described in the foregoing chapter is excellent, however it is well advised to have some additional methods at your command.

THE SYDNEY FLOWER METHOD

Have the subject seated in a chair directly in front of you. Your own chair should be a trifle higher than his so his eyes have to look upwards into yours. Have the chairs close enough together so your knees touch. His hands should lie on his thighs. Now, look him straight in the eyes and take the first joint of the middle finger of each of his hands between the thumb and forefinger of your hands. Forefinger underneath his middle fingers and thumbs above. Hold his hands firmly in this position. Now state to the subject:

> "I .. am .. going .. to .. count .. from .. one .. to .. fifty. Each .. time .. I .. count .. I .. want .. you .. to .. close .. your .. eyes .. and .. open .. them .. between .. counts .. always .. looking .. at .. my .. eyes .. when .. you .. open .. them. Think .. of .. nothing .. but .. sleep .. and .. when .. you .. cannot .. open .. your .. eyes .. anymore .. just .. keep .. them .. closed. Now .. ready! one .. two .. three .. etc.."

At the same time you are counting and the subject is opening and closing his eyes in the rhythm of the count, press your thumb and forefinger together, squeezing the first joints of his middle finger with considerable pressure. Continue this pressure on and off with each count as subject's eyes open and close and continue to gaze into your eyes. Perform this process smoothly and in harmony.

This method will place many people into hypnotic sleep by or before the time you have counted as far as twenty. It is rarely necessary to go the full distance of fifty. If he is not in trance by the time you reach fifty, start over again.

HYPNOTIZING BY TELEPHONE

For this purpose, select a subject you have previously hypnotized. Call him on the phone and tell him to place a chair near the receiver and be seated. Then ask him if he recognizes your voice. If he replies "yes", say to him:

> *"This .. is .. (mention your name). In .. a .. few .. minutes .. you .. will .. be .. sound .. asleep .. in .. deep .. hypnosis. You .. are .. becoming .. so .. sleepy .. you .. can .. not .. keep .. awake. Your .. eyes .. are .. closing .. now .. you .. are .. asleep .. in .. profound .. hypnosis. You .. will .. remain .. sleeping .. comfortably .. in .. your .. chair .. until .. I .. come .. over .. to .. your .. place .. and .. awaken .. you."*

If other arrangements are in order, such as your not being able to call on him personally, give him a suggestion as to the length of time he should remain in trance, such as one hour, and that he will awaken at the end of that time and feel fine.

HYPNOTIZING BY MAIL

Hypnotize subject and have him open his eyes. Show him a specimen of your handwriting. Tell him he will always remember that handwriting. Then awaken him. You can now at any time mail him a letter and when he reads it he will at once become hypnotized. Write this note, as an example:

Dear (name of subject),

While reading this letter you will get very sleepy ... drowsy ... sleepy ... you are falling fast asleep. You cannot keep awake. You will sleep for thirty minutes. You are asleep now in deep hypnosis. After thirty minutes has past, you will awaken feeling happy and well in every way.

Signed (your name in bold letters)

THE MESMERIC METHOD

Mesmerism is a hypnotizing process developed by Dr. Anton Frederick Mesmer (b. 1734, d. 1815). It is a method of producing hypnosis without verbal suggestion.

Have the subject sit or lie in an easy position. Have him look steadily into your eyes while you steadily return his gaze. Now, start making passes without contact from the head down over the body to the knees if sitting, or to the feet if lying down, within one or two inches of the body. Concentrate your mind upon the subject going into hypnotic sleep as you continue the passes until the subject enters the trance state. Use your WILL.

The Mesmerists believe that a subtle "fluid" emanates from the operator called "Animal Magnetism", which is transferred to the body of the subject by means of passes and the direction of will upon the nervous system. They attribute remarkable cures to this power.

Current research suggests that an electromagnetic field surrounds the body of each person, the influence of which is projected most powerfully from the eyes, breath and hands of the individual. The "fluid" (Animal Magnetism) of Mesmerists being in reality the mingling of these force-fields between operator and subject; the force-field of the operator modifying the force-field of the subject, producing in the latter the trance state as directed by the energy of the projected thought. This is to be regarded as theoretical.

CHAPTER FOURTEEN

INSTANTANEOUS METHODS OF HYPNOTIZING

To be able to hypnotize instantly shows that the hypnotist has become a master of giving suggestion-like commands. Such methods must be given with complete confidence. The entire process is forceful. It is well to learn how to induce hypnotic sleep at first by slower methods; when you have developed complete confidence in your ability to hypnotize, then you can try these methods.

THE EYE CLOSURE METHOD

This method is dominated by the suggestion, *"Close your eyes, you are asleep."* You must give the command in a quick voice. Capture the attention of the subject fully and do not remove your eyes from him until he is in trance. You can then apply the "sleep test" by lifting his arm and suggesting he cannot drop it.

This requires quick action and is very effective. If the subject happens to be seated in a chair, turn towards him quick as a flash and point your finger at him, as you command:

> *"You .. cannot .. get .. up .. from .. the .. chair. You .. cannot .. try .. hard .. as .. you .. will. Try it!"*

After trying a moment, say to him:

"Stop .. trying .. now .. and .. close .. your .. eyes. Your .. eyes .. have .. become .. closed .. so .. tightly .. together .. and .. you .. cannot .. open .. them."

After subject has tried in vain to open his eyes, continue right on:

"Stop .. trying .. now .. and .. go .. fast .. asleep. You .. hear .. nothing .. now .. but .. my .. voice. Your .. head .. is .. falling .. forward .. on .. your .. chest. You .. are .. fast .. asleep .. in .. deep .. hypnosis!"

If the suggestions are given in a quick voice in a positive manner, accompanied by a steady gaze of the eyes to those of the subject, this rapid method of inducing hypnosis works wonderfully.

THE SUDDEN SLEEP METHOD

Use a subject you have hypnotized previously and have him take a seat in a chair. Ask him to look you in the eyes. Look at him steadily for about fifteen seconds without saying a word, then suddenly shout "SLEEP!" positively. Make a pass as you say it with both hands directly before his eyes. His eyes will close and he will drop instantly into hypnosis.

THE CHAIR "BUMP" METHOD

Tell the subject you are going to cause him to fall back into his chair and go to sleep. This is the suggestion.

Have subject stand in front of his chair. Make sure the chair is directly behind him so he can fall back into it safely.

Ask the subject to close his eyes and to concentrate on your suggestions:

> "*Your .. chair .. is .. right .. behind .. you. Think .. of ..
> falling .. back .. into .. it. Already .. you .. feel .. an ..
> impulse .. pulling .. you .. over .. backwards .. to .. sit .. in
> .. that .. chair. You .. are .. going .. to .. fall .. back. Your ..
> knees .. are .. bending .. and .. you .. are .. falling .. back ..
> to .. sit .. in .. that .. chair. Sit .. down .. in .. the .. chair.
> Back .. back .. you .. go. Sit .. down! Sit .. down! Sit ..
> down!"*

The subject will begin to sway, falling backwards. Emphasize that he bend his knees so he can fall right over backwards into his chair. He will drop into his chair with a decided "bump". At the moment he experiences this "bump" in dropping into his chair, shout:

> "*SLEEP! GO .. TO .. SLEEP .. THIS .. INSTANT!*"

The bump causes a jar. Immediately grip the subject's head and rotate it around several times. This deepens the instant hypnosis. Then push his head down into his lap and state:

> "*You .. are .. in .. deep .. hypnosis .. now. Sound .. asleep.*"

CHAPTER FIFTEEN

HYPNOTIZING BY FASCINATION

Have subject seated directly in front of you and tell him to lay his hands on his knees, which should be in contact with yours. Lay your own hands on top of his firmly. Now ask him to look you in the eyes steadily without blinking and to think of going to sleep. Keep gazing at his eyes until they close. Through your eyes as you stare at him, express the command of your thought, i.e. "SLEEP".

The subject will drop into deep hypnosis by this eye fascination method. The look of resignation seen in the subject's eyes just before going to sleep is striking.

This method can be used with advantage by deaf people. They should be given to understand, before hypnotizing, that by your given signal (like touching the neck twice or something similar) they will awaken.

MUSIC AS AN AID TO HYPNOSIS

Using music as a background to your hypnotic induction process will be found effective. Just as the singing of a lullaby by the mother puts the child to sleep, so does soft music lull adults. Use a soft, meditative sort of music such as the kind easily obtained in cassette form from esoteric bookstores. Keep the music soft so it does not intrude upon your verbal "suggestion formula". Used subtly, it aids the induction of trance.

An interesting experiment with music that you can try is to give a subject a posthypnotic suggestion that when a certain piece is played, he will immediately drop down deep in hypnosis.

MECHANICAL DEVICES FOR INDUCING HYPNOSIS

There are various devices available for inducing hypnosis such as revolving spiral discs, strobe lights, whirling mirrors, etc.. These are used as the "fixation object" upon which the subject is requested to concentrate attention.

The subject is requested to be seated in front of the device, which is illuminated in a darkened room, and to concentrate on the device. The principle is the tiring of the optic nerve. After five minutes or so of concentrating attention on the effective instrument, the eyes close and sleep ensues. Tell the subject what is expected and his imagination will do the rest.

Mechanical devices for inducing hypnosis are effective when working with several people at the same time, however for most purposes they are not necessary. As a hypnotist, come to rely on your own personality, not mechanical devices.

HYPNOTIZING WITH A CANDLE

In a sense, hypnotizing using a candle is a "mechanical device" but it is a very subtle one, as candles have long been associated with transcendental and religious ceremonies.

Seat the subject in a chair in a darkened room. Light a candle and set it within two feet of the person's eyes. Set it up high enough so he has to look upward to the flame. Now, make a mark about a half inch (or less) from the top of the candle and tell the subject positively that when the candle has melted down to the mark indicated he will be sound asleep. Impress on him the necessity of watching the flame with both eyes steadily. If he does not close them of his own accord by the time the candle has burned down to the mark, close them for him gently with your thumbs and suggest that they stay closed and he cannot open them, that he is ASLEEP.

Then present a "sleep formula" and make passes without contact over the body of the subject. Hypnosis is soon induced.

Hypnotizing by candlelight will be found an effective method to hypnotize people who find it difficult to concentrate. The flickering flame seems to exert a fascination that is hard to resist.

SELF-HYPNOSIS

It has been said that at its roots, all hypnosis is self-induced. Self-hypnosis is autosuggestion, i.e., if you can implant a suggestion in the mind of someone else, it is logical to assume you can equally implant wanted suggestions (ideas) in your own subconscious mind. For this purpose, lie down, cup your hands over your ears and close your eyes. Relax all muscles and THINK of going to sleep. Commence speaking to yourself out loud like this:

"I .. am .. going .. to .. hypnotize .. myself .. and .. put .. myself .. asleep. I .. am .. becoming .. so .. drowsy .. I .. am .. going .. to .. sleep. I .. am .. so .. drowsy, .. sleepy, .. etc.."

Keep on telling yourself that you are going to sleep and specify the time you wish to awaken. Exclude all other thoughts and concentrate on what you are expecting to accomplish. So be it.

With practice you will find that you can learn to hypnotize yourself anytime you wish and give yourself beneficial suggestions to become your very own. You will find this method of speaking out loud to yourself with hands cupped over your ears very powerful; the suggestions are caused to "ring" inside your head, as it were.

THE PROGRESSIVE RELAXATION INDUCTION

This Self Hypnosis Technique and method called "Progressive Relaxation" is a wonderful technique that will help relax you, revitalize you, and is also a great way to implant your own positive suggestions into your subconscious mind. All you have to do is to find yourself a comfortable chair or recliner to sit on. You can also sit on the floor in a comfortable position. Place your hands face down on your lap, look down at your hands and focus your attention on your breathing. Take three slow deep breaths in and out and think of the word "Relaxation". Hold each breath in for about five seconds before your exhale. As you exhale, imagine yourself relaxing a different part of your body, such as relaxing the muscles in your toes and feet. Relaxing the muscles in your stomach, or relaxing your shoulders and back, or relaxing the muscles around your eyelids etc. On your fifth exhale, close your eyes and imagine a wave of relaxation moving from the top of your head all the way down to the tips of your toes. Now imagine with your eyes still closed, that you are in a beautiful place or relaxation, like lying on a beach, in a meadow, at the park, by a stream or mountain or some other place of beauty and peace. Just imagine yourself really there and use your child like imagination or even just pretend that you are there. Once you are there, then it is time to give yourself positive suggestions such as, "I'm a happy person", "I love myself ", I'm a success in everything I do", "I have lot's of energy", "I am calm and relaxed", or give yourself, your own positive suggestions. To awaken, simply count to yourself from one up to five, and then say to yourself out loud a few times, "I'm wide awake with lot's of energy"! Open your eyes and wake up with a big smile.

CHAPTER SIXTEEN

HYPNOTIC INDUCTIONS FOR GROUP HYPNOSIS

Especially in presenting stage demonstrations of hypnotism will group hypnosis be employed. Here are three methods of hypnotizing any number of persons at the same time:

METHOD ONE

Seat subjects in a semicircle. Give each one a bright coin to hold and tell them to look at it without moving their eyes from the shiny coin for even an instant. Then stand to one side and after a few minutes say:

> "As .. you .. stare .. at .. the .. shiny .. coin .. your .. eyes .. are .. getting .. heavy .. you .. cannot .. keep .. them .. open .. any .. longer ... they .. are .. closing .. closing .. now .. and .. you .. are .. becoming .. so .. drowsy .. and .. sleepy. Go .. to .. sleep .. now, .. etc."

Give sleep formula until they are all in hypnotic sleep.

METHOD TWO

Have the subjects seated in a semicircle. Stand in the center before them. Now say:

> "Look .. me .. straight .. in .. the .. eyes .. and .. think .. of .. sleep. " (Look from one to another and then straight ahead and it will seem to each you are looking

straight at him.) *"Now .. close .. your .. eyes .. and .. as .. I .. count .. up .. to .. ten .. you .. find .. your .. heads .. are .. getting .. heavy .. and .. you .. will .. be .. sound .. asleep. One .. two .. three .. four .. five .. six .. seven .. eight .. nine .. TEN. Fast .. asleep .. sound .. asleep .. sleepy .. drowsy .. fast .. asleep. Your .. heads .. are .. so .. heavy .. you .. cannot .. hold .. them .. up .. any .. longer. You .. are .. fast .. asleep."*

Continue these suggestions until all heads of persons in the group fall over and rest on chests. Go to each person in turn and place your hand on top of their head as you exclaim, *"SLEEP!"*. You have hypnotized the group. Some may even fall off their chair. Each will act according to their nature.

METHOD THREE

The mechanical device of the revolving mirror is used in this method. Place it on a stand in the center of a group seated in a semicircle. Start it going and tell them to watch it and never to remove their eyes from it. In a few minutes, give suggestions for closing of the eyes; then proceed into "sleep formula". After they are in trance, remove the mirror and you are ready to give performance suggestions.

HOW TO DEEPEN THE HYPNOTIC SLEEP

Having hypnotized the group, with all heads resting forward on chests, you can deepen the hypnotic sleep by these methods:

80

"Breathe .. in .. deeply .. now. Inhale (pause) .. Exhale (pause) .. Breathe .. in .. deep .. and .. free .. and .. every .. breath .. you .. take .. will .. cause .. you .. to .. go .. deeper .. and .. deeper .. into .. hypnosis. Deep .. deep .. to .. sleep. Fast .. asleep."

Go to each subject in turn and lift up their right hand as you state:

"When .. I .. release .. your .. hand .. it .. will .. fall .. directly .. to .. your .. lap .. and .. when .. it .. falls .. into .. your .. lap .. you .. will .. be .. fast .. asleep .. in .. deep .. hypnosis."

Go to each subject in turn and lift up their hand by gripping the thumb. Let their hand dangle for a moment from the thumb and then release the thumb so that their hand drops into their lap. The moment it hits their lap, state forcefully:

"SLEEP! YOU ARE DEEP ASLEEP!"

Another method of deepening hypnosis is to go to each subject in turn and start revolving their head around and around as you state:

"Each .. revolution .. of .. your .. head .. sends .. you .. down .. deeper .. and .. deeper .. into .. hypnotic .. sleep. SLEEP .. DEEP. You .. are .. in .. profound .. hypnosis."

Hypnotized college student performs a full body "catalepsy" by
becoming stiff and rigid as a "steel bar". November 1988

CHAPTER SEVENTEEN

HOW TO PRODUCE HYPNOTIC ANESTHESIA

Pain in the body can be controlled by the mind. Hypnosis provides the means to numb pain using direct suggestions.

Put the subject in as deep a state of hypnosis as possible. Now make a few passes over the spot and then press your hands firmly on the spot in the body where the pain is felt. Press in until the person complains, then release the pressure, but still allow your hand to rest on that spot while you give these direct suggestions:

> "The .. place .. upon .. your .. body .. on .. which .. my .. hand .. is .. resting .. is .. becoming .. numb. All .. sensation .. in .. that .. spot .. is .. becoming .. numb. All .. sensation .. in .. that .. spot .. even .. when .. I .. pinch .. your .. skin .. you .. feel .. nothing .. at .. all. It .. is .. insensible. It .. is .. anesthetized."

Repeat these suggestions in a forceful manner three times. Then give the subject's skin (over the spot which pains) a sharp pinch. If nothing is felt, anesthesia has set in.

When possible, do not mention the word "pain" when giving suggestions to remove pain. Center your suggestions on numbness and insensibility.

FOR DENTAL WORK

Hypnotize subject a few times (each induction following the other rapidly) before the dentist starts operating. This handling is known as pyramiding. It produces a deep state

83

of hypnosis. When you know the subject is deeply entranced, suggest:

"You .. will .. do .. everything .. your .. dentist .. tells .. you .. to .. do .. perfectly. Your .. mouth .. is .. insensible. It .. feels .. absolutely .. numb. Just .. have .. a .. peaceful .. sleep .. while .. your .. dentist .. fixes .. your .. teeth."

Occasionally during the dental session, suggest to the patient:

"You .. are .. having .. a .. pleasant .. snooze .. while .. your .. dentist .. works .. on .. your .. teeth. You .. feel .. nothing .. in .. your .. mouth. You .. will .. just .. sleep .. on .. until .. I .. tell .. you .. it .. is .. time .. to .. awaken."

When the dental operation is complete, tell the patient he will feel fine when he awakens and will recall nothing whatsoever of the dental session.

COMPLETE BODY ANESTHESIA

After a deep state of hypnosis has been produced, take each part of the body and suggest anesthesia separately to them. Do not simply tell the subject that his whole body is without feeling, as that is too general. Make passes over each part and press in with your hand when suggesting insensibility in each part until arms, legs, head, shoulders, chest, torso and lower limbs are included in the anesthesia.

ANESTHESIA IN THE WAKING STATE

Hypnotic sleep is not always necessary to produce a condition of analgesia in a subject. Absence of pain can be suggested very often in the waking state. Physicians can use this method in trifling operations performed in the office. A placebo method is applied using indirect suggestions. In such instances, the doctor may say to the subject:

"Mr. Jones (subject's name), I .. have .. here .. a .. new .. form .. of .. anesthetic .. which .. has .. recently .. been .. developed. It .. works .. very .. rapidly .. and .. will .. completely .. remove .. any .. sense .. from .. the .. area .. upon .. which .. I .. will .. perform .. this .. very .. minor .. operation. You .. will .. find .. it .. will .. make .. the .. area .. absolutely .. numb."

A little of the imaginary anesthetic is then rubbed on the spot. A few moments of waiting and then the physician proceeds. Remarkably, the patient feels nothing.

To successfully use this process, the physician must have knowledge of how to give positive suggestions. Three essentials must work in harmony: the voice should be even toned and positive, the suggestions must be positive and definite, and the physician must have the confidence of knowing what he says will be believed. As an example, suppose it is desired to induce analgesia in the hand of a patient; go about it in this manner:

Take the patient's hand in your left hand. Look him squarely in the eyes. Do not blink and hold his attention on the eyes. Stroke his hand with your right hand a few times. Now say to him:

"Your .. hand .. has .. no .. feeling .. in .. it .. at .. all. It .. is .. numb .. and .. insensible. See, .. even .. when .. I .. pinch .. the .. skin .. you .. feel .. nothing .. at .. all."

The whole secret is positive suggestions and concentration of will on what is being done. Even the flow of blood can often be controlled, as a few suggestions will verify. Repeat suggestions a few times in every case.

BODY SUSPENSION CATALEPSY

To induce a rigid condition of the muscles in the whole body, put the subject to sleep while standing up. Tell him to throw his chest forward as much as possible and take a firm grip of his trousers on each side of his body and make his body as stiff as possible. With your right hand, raise up his head, look sharply in the eyes and suggest as follows:

> "You .. are .. going .. sound .. asleep. Fast .. asleep, .. and .. when .. I .. count .. three .. all .. the .. muscles .. in .. your .. body .. will .. become .. stiff .. and .. rigid .. like .. an .. iron .. bar. One .. two .. three, .. your .. body .. is .. stiff .. like .. a .. bar .. of .. iron. It .. is .. rigid .. and .. will .. not .. bend."

While giving these suggestions, make passes down his sides from head to toes, occasionally touching head, arms, chest and legs. Have someone hold him steady from behind. Now ask someone to take his shoulders and someone else to take hold of his feet and lay him outstretched across the back of two chairs or wooden sawhorses. Any supports used should be cushions and the subject's shoulders should be well up on the chair back. The ankles should rest on the other chair. Have a person sit on each chair facing the subject and tell them to hold on so he won't slip. Then drape a heavy cloth over his body, covering him from shoulders to feet. With your right hand, raise him up in the middle and again suggest:

"Stiff .. rigid .. stiff .. your .. body .. is .. like .. a .. bar .. of .. iron."

Then try sitting on his suspended body and, if he holds your weight, you can stand on him. After completing the feat, have your assistants remove him from chair backs and stand him upright on his feet, then say:

"Relax .. your .. muscles .. now. Relax .. your .. body .. in .. every .. way. When .. I .. count .. three .. you .. will .. awaken .. and .. feel .. just .. fine. One .. two .. three. All .. right. You .. are .. wide .. awake .. and .. feel .. just .. fine."

Be very positive when making suggestions in this experiment. It is often used as a sensational demonstration in hypnotism stage shows.

PRODUCING THE LONG TRANCE

This experiment is rarely conducted and should be attempted only under professional supervision. In such instance, the hypnotized subject remains in the trance for as long as forty-eight hours without difficulty.

The subject used should be a person who readily enters profound hypnosis and should not eat or drink anything before breakfast. In other words, his stomach should be empty in performing this experiment. Hypnotize him in a deep trance, suggesting that he can hear nothing but your voice and nothing will disturb him or awaken him. Tell him he will sleep comfortably for forty-eight hours and that he cannot awaken beforehand, but between the forty-eighth and forty-ninth hours he will awaken easily by counting up to ten, and he will feel fine in having had a wonderful, healthful sleep which will have benefited his body in every way.

Suggest to him that during his sleep he will not feel hungry or thirsty, all functions of his body are suspended except breathing and heart action, the functioning of his organs will be perfectly normal, he cannot move, and will be perfectly comfortable during his long trance.

Specify the length of his sleep and insist that he cannot awaken beforehand unless you awaken him. Lay great stress on this point. Suggest to him that in case an accident should happen to you in the meantime, he will awaken at a certain specified time (which you must state) of his own accord. Never forget this! Repeat each suggestion at least three times positively.

When you are ready to awaken him from the long trance, have three or four persons hold him firmly until he is fully aroused. Some subjects fight for a few minutes on being brought out of the trance and it is best to be prepared. Only an excellent hypnotic subject should be used for this experiment.

Prolonged hypnosis has been used as a therapy in cases of nervous disorders caused by pronounced body stress. It gives the body much needed time and space for recovery.

美國催眠大師湯姆表演催眠
李玟回到前世體驗「死生」

△李玟被催眠大師湯姆催眠，引領至前世。

Tom Silver "shocks" Taiwan by hypnotizing famous Taiwan celebrity singer, Coco, into past life memory. Taipei, Taiwan, R.O.C..
September 1994

CHAPTER EIGHTEEN

HYPNOSIS AND PSYCHIC PHENOMENA

Many people are interested in the psychic aspects of mind. Studies in Extra Sensory Perception (ESP) are being scientifically conducted. Hypnosis can enhance these powers. This chapter is devoted to such consideration.

EXPERIMENTING WITH CLAIRVOYANCE

Clairvoyance is the psychic ability to envision occurrences at a distance. The intervening space as related to miles has no meaning to the phenomena. Some people seem to have the faculty of spontaneous clairvoyance. A good hypnotic subject may be developed into a clairvoyant by experimenting along these lines. It takes persistence. Use this method:

Put the subject into as deep a trance as you can and then continue to make passes over him for fifteen minutes longer while concentrating your mind on his developing such powers. Use passes without contact and the more profound the hypnosis induced the better. Work in a darkened room when possible. When he is in a deep trance, try this experiment:

Write a single number (from 1 to 10) on a slip of paper. Take the paper in the palm of your hand and press it on the top of his head. Ask him to tell you what the number is using these suggestions:

"I want you to tell me what number, from one to ten, I have written on this slip of paper I am now holding to your head. You can see it perfectly in your mind's eye. It is

getting plainer to your inner vision all the time. SEE IT NOW!"

Insist that he can see it. Be very positive and command him to see. If he does not at first, make more passes and quickly say to him:

"NOW YOU SEE IT!"

If the entranced subject names the number correctly, then try it with two numbers, then three, and so on. This is all part of initial clairvoyant training. Then take an object, like a book or whatever, and have him describe it as he envisions it within his mind.

Do not expect too much at first but by persistent practice he will develop wonderfully. Of course, all hypnotic subjects will not show clairvoyant talent but when you find a person with the gift, hypnotically experiment with him for that purpose only.

Clairvoyance is an elusive phenomena. On some days it will be surprisingly accurate while at other times nothing seems to come through. But be persistent in your experiments with a clairvoyant subject. After being successful with numbers and different objects in the same room in which you are experimenting, then ask him to describe some place at a distance with which you are familiar. Then have him describe a distant place he sees within his mind with which neither of you are familiar.

Remember, clairvoyance is a psychic talent which must be developed and practice makes perfect. When accuracy comes in along with the phenomena, results can be amazing.

EXPERIMENTING WITH CLAIRAUDIENCE

Clairvoyance is a term meaning "clear psychic seeing". Clairaudience means "clear psychic hearing". Some persons are more visually minded while others are more related to hearing. In relation to experimenting with these psychic talents of the mind, use whatever approach works best for the subject. If his perceptions come in through a sense of hearing, such as an inner voice speaking to him inside himself, use an auditory approach to your experiments. Some subjects perform excellently when directed through clairaudience.

EXPERIMENTING WITH TELEPATHY

Telepathy seems to be an inherent power in man to communicate his thoughts to others independent of objective means of communication. A state of mental quiescence (mental passivity) seems to be the most favorable condition for the reception of telepathic impressions and communications. As hypnosis can induce perfect passivity, it is excellent to use for telepathic experimenting.

Induce in a subject as deep a hypnotic state as possible. Blindfold the subject to exclude all light. Then write on a piece of paper a mental request you wish the subject to perform. Start with some simple test such as pointing to some object on the table of which you are thinking. Possibly start with thinking of salt, pepper, sugar and vinegar. Place a sample of one of these on your tongue and ask the subject to tell what taste is experienced. The sense of taste often is a good one to start with in telepathic experimenting.

When you develop a good telepathic rapport with a subject, you will find you can almost seem to direct the person to perform different acts that you mentally command, i.e. acts performed without saying a word.

When you find you have a subject with whom you have a telepathic rapport, then experiment together over a distance. Distance has no meaning at all to thought. You can attempt hypnotizing the person at a distance. Try this:

Relax yourself in a comfortable chair at a time of night in which the distant subject is likely to be asleep. Now blindfold your eyes to eliminate all light and concentrate your mind on the distant person. Think of nothing else in your mind but the person and give a mental command that such will be carried out by the person as having originated in his own mind. For example, think of him and repeat his name to yourself, saying, *"John Doe, you will come to my house tomorrow at 8:00 p.m.. You will come. I want you to come."* Repeat this mental direction to yourself ten times or so while you are establishing this distant communication with the subjects. The mental command will often be followed exactly as you have telepathically communicated it. Results can be startling.

EXPERIMENTING WITH DISTANT HEALING

Various religious practices make use of distant healing. A time for the treatment is arranged between healer and subject. The subject is to recline at that specified time and become passive and receptive to the healing influence that the practitioner will send to him. At the appointed time, the healer also becomes passive and visualizes the subject as being close, then sends positive thoughts mentally to the person to affect a cure of whatever the trouble may be. The suggestions in the form of thought waves are thus received by the subject's subjective mind and inasmuch as the latter has absolute control of all the functions of the body and is amenable to the control by suggestion (whether oral or mental), a cure of the difficulty is often obtained. The essential part of cure is the earnestness of purpose on the part of the healer and a passive condition of willingness of the subject.

Also, elements of faith and belief are important in such treatment. As Christ so succinctly put it, "Believe ye in me and ye will be healed".

All such psychic phenomena of mind must be looked upon as EXPERIMENTING WITH EXPERIENCING.

CHAPTER NINETEEN

MISCELLANEOUS HYPNOTIC THINGS YOU SHOULD KNOW

GAINING LOVE AND RESPECT

Put the subject back into deep hypnosis and give the following suggestions in a positive and forceful manner as you place your hands on his head with your thumb at the root of his nose:

> *"A strong bond of friendship is developing between us. We love and respect each other. You will have confidence in me as I have in you. You love and respect me. You will strongly sense this bond of love, respect and friendship flowing between us when you awaken from hypnosis."*

Repeat these suggestions three times. Then let him remain silently in hypnosis for about five minutes before arousing. The harmonizing effects between people of such positive suggestion functioning on the posthypnotic level are remarkable.

ALTERATION OF CHARACTER

Hypnosis provides a wonderful way to motivate and improve the character of a person. For example, if a person is inclined to be lazy and restless to succeed in life, you can alter that disposition remarkably by the use of posthypnotic suggestions.

Secure the subject's consent to improve his character and send him into deep hypnosis. Then give these suggestions a half dozen times or so:

> *"From now on, you will work steadily, you will not care to change positions every few days, you will be filled with the ambition to succeed. It will be a pleasure for you to work every day, earn your own way and be a success in business and your life. By doing this, you will become a credit to your community and your country and everyone will like you and speak of you highly. When I arouse you from this hypnotic trance, you will not remember that I have given you these suggestions but you will do exactly as I have told you, and you will imagine that it is your own impulse and idea. You are headed towards success, now and forever more."*

Let him remain in hypnosis for ten minutes and then awaken him.

THE TIME FACTOR IN POSTHYPNOSIS

An interesting experiment in posthypnosis is to suggest to a subject, while deep in hypnosis:

> *"You will have a strong impulse to come to my house at 8:00 p.m. on the dot one week from today. You won't know why ... you will simply say you had an impulse to come for a visit."*

Repeat six times. Then awaken the subject. Arousing from deep hypnosis, he will have no memory of the suggestions you have given him, but in one week he will be on your porch ringing your doorbell at 8:00 p.m..

A response to a posthypnotic suggestion will often occur as a surprise to the subject. He will remember nothing until the time comes and then he will respond to the suggestions spontaneously as though it were his own idea. It makes no difference as to the length of intervening period from when the suggestion was given and its ultimate summation. It may be a day, a week, a month, a year or sometimes even longer.

The mind has an amazing sense of time. An experiment was tried in which a young lady, age nineteen, was told she would draw the sign of the cross on the sidewalk in front of her house after the lapse of 4,335 minutes. In spite of the fact that she had forgotten all about the suggestions, she fulfilled it accurately and drew the cross precisely on the minute.

HOW TO REGULATE A SUBJECT'S HEART BEAT

The subconscious is a remarkable regulator of body functions. Try putting a subject into deep hypnosis and suggest:

> "When .. I .. count .. three .. your .. heart .. will .. beat .. faster .. faster .. faster. One .. two .. three. Your .. heart .. is .. beating .. faster .. faster .. faster."

Keep track of your subject's pulse rate and you will see that your suggestions are being responded to. To decrease pulsation, tell him that his pulse is beating slower, slower, slower. You will get a very slow pulse beat. Before awakening, restore the subject to his normal rate of heart pulsation. Never use a subject with a weak heart for this experiment!

CAUSING TWO DIFFERENT PULSE BEATS IN THE SAME SUBJECT

Normally this is considered an impossibility, but it can be done when a person is in profound hypnosis. Start by inducing a sleep state and suggest catalepsy of the entire body. Then suggest as follows:

> "When .. I .. count .. ten .. your .. whole .. body .. will .. become .. stiff .. and .. rigid. It .. is .. like .. a .. stone. You .. cannot .. bend .. a .. muscle. You .. are .. absolutely .. calm .. and .. your .. body .. is becoming .. colder .. and .. your .. heartbeat .. is .. slowing .. down. Slow .. slow .. slower."

Suggest until you get a plus reading of, say, sixty beats per minute. Now take hold of the right arm and suggest:

> "This .. arm .. is .. going .. to .. remain .. cold .. and .. the .. pulse .. beat .. remains .. the .. same. The .. rest .. of .. your .. body .. is .. relaxing .. and .. will .. get .. warm .. and .. the .. pulse .. in .. your .. other .. arm .. will .. beat .. faster .. faster .. faster."

Now check the pulses in both wrists and you can note a difference sometimes ranging from as much as fifteen to twenty beats per minute. To end the experiment, return the heart beat to normal, beating equally in each arm.

Again, to repeat, do not perform any experiment of this physiological nature upon any persons with a weak heart!

RAISING A BLISTER BY HYPNOTIC SUGGESTION

Hypnotize subject deeply and say you are going to place a very hot piece of metal upon his skin. Tell him it will not harm him or cause him any pain, but it will cause the skin beneath the spot on which the hot metal was placed to become red, inflamed, and will raise a harmless blister on that spot.

Then place a coin on the skin and press it there. Hold for some five minutes. Continue to suggest:

> *"It is hot and will raise a blister on your skin, but it does not bother you in any way and the blister will soon go away."*

This is experimental. With some subjects, the results are remarkable and a blister appears on the skin when the coin is removed.

After observing the effect, rub the spot and say:

> *"It is all cool now ... your skin is cool and the blister is going away."*

This experiment shows clearly the power mind has over body functioning. Skin is especially responsive to suggestions. The phenomena could well put a new light on the appearance of "stigmata".

CHAPTER TWENTY

MOVING ON TO SUGGESTIVE THERAPEUTICS AND HYPNOTHERAPY

As mind affects the body, just as body affects the mind, in a circling of influence, it is entirely possible to aid in the treatment of physical ailments as well as psychological ones with hypnotherapy, as you will learn in this chapter. However, the hypnotherapist must not invade the domain of the physician. He works with clients, never patients, and never diagnoses.

During the Victorian Age on through the 1920's, what you will now study was called "suggestive therapeutics". Today, hypnosis used for therapeutic purposes is called "hypnotherapy" and is recognized by the American Medical Association (AMA) as a valuable ally in the treatment of disease (dis-ease).

Hypnosis used as hypnotherapy is unquestionably its most important usefulness. The mind of the hypnotized person being in a subjective state is ready to accept any and all suggestions as true, provided they are not in conflict with his moral nature. The hypnotist must remember this rule:

The strongest suggestion implanted in the subject's subconscious rules the roost.

Unless otherwise directed, the subject is in rapport with the operator only, and he readily accepts suggestions from that source as they are given him.

Hypnotherapy employs posthypnotic suggestions beneficial to the subject, which are usually complied with following awakening or sometime later, as directed. Many persons have been cured of physical and mental distress without the aid of medicine using the process. The major requirement being that the client be willing to be cured of his ailment, in cooperation with his therapist.

We will now describe in detail a number of diseases which appear to respond to hypnotic suggestion. Every disease is treated in practically the same manner. All that is necessary is to word your suggestions POSITIVELY! You must learn how to give suggestions positively with conviction and precision. Practice to do so. Here's an exercise you can use:

Go into a private room by yourself and talk out loud to an empty chair, table or whatever you wish to talk to. It makes no difference. Its only purpose is to provide you with a personal exercise to present suggestions most effectively. Suggestions that are most effective are suggestions that influence and suggestions that most influence are invariable POSITIVE SUGGESTIONS!

To help cure a person of an ailment, it is often not necessary to induce hypnotic sleep, as a suggestion properly presented in the waking state will greatly benefit. In hypnotherapy, a good deal depends on your prehypnotic suggestions (consultation) given the patient when he applies for treatment. If you can inspire in him faith and confidence in your ability to help him, you have advanced already towards the cure.

Never state impossibilities in relation to "miracles" occurring, but affirm you can definitely be a great help, as testified by the many people you have helped.

In relation to hypnotherapy, never tell the patient that profound hypnosis will be necessary to his cure. Tell him honestly that there are many different stages of hypnosis and it makes little difference whether he enters a light stage or a deep stage. Your treatment will benefit him just the same.

If you wish, you can tell the client of some of the cases you have treated, similar to his own that have been greatly benefited. Your aim is to establish confidence that you can aid him. If he should ask how long it will take to cure him, tell him one cannot tell; some clients respond fully in only one session while others take two or three. It all depends on the nature of the disease and the responsiveness of the client to your suggestions, whatever such may be.

In hypnotherapy, you have no opportunity to be selective of those who seek your service. As you are able, induce as deep a state of hypnosis as is possible but be willing to work with whatever depth of hypnosis the client enters into. And now, let's consider how to handle some specific types of diseases that respond well to hypnotherapy.

THE TREATING OF ARTHRITIS

Put the client in as deep a state of hypnosis as you can. Now say to him:

> "When I awaken you, you will find that the pain in your arms (or whatever part of the body his pain is in) has entirely disappeared. You will not be troubled with arthritis any longer. The blood will flow strongly through your arm which will cause all poison to scatter and relieve your pain. You can use your arm perfectly and free from pain. When you awaken and come back to here and now, you will never be bothered with arthritis again."

Make some passes over the part affected and repeat these suggestions eight or ten times very positively. Awaken him by a slow and gentle method.

In this operation, be sure to find out before inducing hypnosis the exact nature of his trouble and the very spot where the pain exists. Then centralize your suggestions to that location. Repeating of suggestions has a compounding effect on mastering the disease. In hypnotherapy, always repeat suggestions eight or ten times in a positive, earnest, convincing manner. Put your heart and soul into the work. A strong will and desire will accomplish wonders.

THE TREATING OF HEADACHE

Put the client as deeply into hypnosis as possible. Then place your hand on his forehead and suggest:

> *"When you awaken, your headache will have disappeared. You will feel fine. You will even have forgotten that you had a headache. It has entirely disappeared."*

Repeat these suggestions at least eight times. Then slowly awaken the client. Most clients will find they have forgotten all about their headache.

Another method for treating a headache is to take a clean pocket handkerchief and fold it over a number of times forming a pad. Place this pad over the spot on the head where the headache is. Then place your open mouth in the center of the pad and blow warm air from your lungs upon the folded handkerchief. It will become very warm through this process. Ten minutes of such treatment often cures the most pronounced headache.

THE TREATING OF NEURALGIA

Induce as deep a hypnotic state as possible. Then say to the client:

"You are relaxing more and more ... so go ahead and drop down into the realm of sleep. And when you awaken, your neuralgia will have disappeared. Your face is free of all pain. Nothing will trouble you and you are fine."

Make some passes over the affected part while giving suggestions and awaken slowly. So simple. Almost hard to believe. Just a few words given in the hypnotic state and the pain is gone and health is on its way. Simple? Not really. The subconscious mind is beyond doubt the most remarkable mechanism you possess.

THE TREATING OF EARACHE

Induce as deep a hypnotic state as possible. Then place your hand on the affected ear and suggest:

"This trouble in your ear is leaving you. When you awaken, your earache will be GONE! You will feel fine. The trouble is gone forever."

In giving therapeutic suggestions, do not hold back. State exactly what you want to occur. Expect the cure to be effective. So be it!

You can treat a toothache in the same manner as in curing an earache. Place your hands on the client's jaw and suggest:

"The pain is gone. You feel all well and fine."

THE TREATING OF INDIGESTION

Have client lie upon a couch or bed outstretched and hypnotize him as deeply as you can. Then suggest:

> *"From now on you will have no more trouble with your stomach."* (Place your hand on his stomach.) *"The food you eat will digest perfectly. No gas will form in the stomach anymore. The blood will flow to your stomach and you will be able to eat anything you wish. Each day your digestion will function better and better in every way."*

Give these suggestions over eight or ten times before awakening the subject. He should be treated every day for about a week if he has chronic indigestion.

THE TREATING OF GENERAL DEBILITY

Always find out what ails your client in detail. Have him describe the symptoms several times so as to learn them by heart. To treat this malady, have the client lie down and put him into trance in this position. Then suggest:

> *"When I awaken you and from today on, you will feel very much improved. You will feel stronger. Your appetite will increase. You will enjoy three good square meals a day. Your bowels will move regularly every day. Your strength will increase every hour. You are becoming stronger and better in every way. In fact, when I awaken you now, you will feel better in every way."*

Make passes over the client from head to foot, ten or twelve times. Always tell your client, before you awaken him, that each time you work together he will go deeper and deeper into hypnotic sleep for the purpose of treating him for the benefit of his health. In this way, you will condition him to hypnosis and he will quickly enter the state so you can best aid him. Then awaken him.

THE TREATING OF BACKACHE

Induce as deep a state of hypnosis as possible, then suggest:

> *"When I awaken you, all the pain in your back will be gone. You will feel well and fine. You will be able to walk straight and will have no pain whatsoever. You will sleep well at night and will feel rested when you arise in the morning.   Your kidneys will perform their duties to perfection.   Any aching in your back has completely disappeared."*

Place your hands on his back and press in on the spot where the pain occurs. Then awaken him.

THE TREATING OF HEART CONDITION

Never use any bright object when hypnotizing to treat a heart condition.   Use a gentle progressive relaxation method. In every way, make the patient calm and serene. Induce as deep a state of hypnosis as you can and suggest:

> *"Now you are becoming calm and relaxed all over. Your heartbeat is perfectly normal, as is your blood pressure. Your heart is completely free of pain.   Your heart is functioning normally just as it is supposed to do. Every time I treat you, you will become better.   You improve*

every day. You are well and fine. When I awaken you, you will be well and fine."

Place your hand over his heart as you give these suggestions and awaken him very slowly. Whatever the nature of his heart trouble may be, give suggestions to counteract this.

THE TREATING OF CONSTIPATION

Believe it or not, this condition is often at the bottom of all other ailments and special attention should be given to it. The client should always be asked for his condition as regards to constipation. Hypnotize the client and give the following suggestions:

> *"Tomorrow morning at six o'clock* (a convenient time should be specified), *you will awaken from your natural sleep and go to the bathroom and your bowels will move perfectly. Remember, at six o'clock* (time specified), *you will have a strong desire to do as I have told you. You cannot resist it."*

Repeat these suggestions a half dozen times and lay great stress on the exact time when the bowel movement will occur. Continue:

> *"You will from now on every morning go to the bathroom at the same time and have a bowel movement. You will also drink a glass of water before breakfast every morning. Remember this. Every morning before breakfast you will drink a glass of water. In a few days, your bowels will be in a normal condition again and able to throw off all*

poisons to your system and you will commence to feel better in every way."

Repeat these suggestions for ten minutes before awakening him. Always speak plainly so the client knows exactly what you mean. Three or four such treatments usually cure the worse cases of constipation.

THE TREATING OF INSOMNIA

After inducing hypnosis, suggest:

"At ten o'clock tonight and every night thereafter you will get so sleepy that you cannot stay awake and no matter where you are you will go at once to your home and go to bed. You will go to sleep right away and you will sleep soundly all night long. You will not awaken until six or seven (give normal awakening time) *in the morning. Every night from now on you will sleep and rest wonderfully and well and nothing will disturb your sleep in anyway."*

Be sure to specify the time in the evening and morning so as not to interfere with his business hours. Treat him every day until he sleeps well at night. His insomnia is gone.

THE TREATING OF PARALYSIS

This sometimes requires a bit of rough handling.
Put the person into deep hypnosis. Should his legs be paralyzed, take both hands and, after removing clothing, start to slap them briskly until the flesh gets red and manipulate them vigorously. Be forceful in your handling

108

such clients and, while doing so, give suggestions that he can walk without difficulty, that all his lameness is gone. Have him open his eyes (do not awaken him from the hypnosis) and command him to get up and walk around. If he says he cannot, pay no attention but insist that he can walk. Make him get up and do so. Before you awaken him, give him very positive suggestions that after he awakens he will be able to walk without difficulty. Repeat your suggestions a dozen times. Be insistent that he can walk. Treat him every day. He may be cured in one treatment or it may take many but never give up.

COOPERATION WITH THE PHYSICIAN

As a hypnotherapist, remember your place is to be an adjunct to the physician. You do not replace the doctor. Cooperate and work with the physician. He has his ways of curing and you have yours. Together, remarkable results in curing human ills can be achieved.

NOTE: Most cases in working with physical ailments by the hypnotherapist are in response to physician recommendation as supplemental treatment or via direct referral. The same applies to the Magnetic Healing methods which you will learn in Chapter Twenty-Three.

Actor, Alan Rosenberg, is hypnotized by Tom Silver into stopping smoking on the national television show, "The Home and Family Show," starring Chuck Woolery and Christine Ferara. May 1996

110

CHAPTER TWENTY-ONE

MASTERING UNWANTED HABITS

Habits can be good or bad. We want the good ones and are better off without the bad ones. Habits are usually based in bringing some kind of pleasure to the user. Once habits become solidly established as a way of behavior for the individual, they enter the realm of the subconscious and operate beyond critical thought. Hence, since hypnosis provides a direct means of controlling the subconscious, it provides an excellent means of getting rid of unwanted habits. And since habits are mainly based on a pleasure response for the individual, all that is needed to get rid of them is to reverse pleasure for displeasure. With this understanding, here are suggestion formulas for the control of habits that you can use with your clients in hypnotherapy.

In treating habits, suggestions related to the particular habit must be used. The essential thing is to repeat each suggestion many times to produce a counter "mental set" to the habit. Cures are effectively obtained by repeating of the anti-habit suggestions over and over. Patience and not haste is the essential requirement for successful treatments of unwanted (often vicious) habits.

For any form of unwanted habit to be removed, its removal must commence on the conscious desire of the one who has the habit to have it removed.

MASTERING THE DRINKING HABIT

Before hypnotizing the client to master the drinking habit, find out the quantity of liquor he daily consumes. This done, hypnotize him and suggest:

"From now on you will only drink half of what you have been used to drinking. If you try to drink one glass more than that, it will taste like vinegar to you. You cannot drink any more than that. Every day you will care less for whisky, beer, wine and liquor of any kind. Any drink with alcohol in it is losing its appeal to you. You will learn to hate it. It will make you sick to drink it. All craving for alcoholic drinks of any kind is leaving you. You have no desire for it anymore and the habit is leaving you. You will sleep well nights and you have no desire at all for liquor in the morning."

Repeat to the hypnotized client these suggestions for twenty minutes. Do not tell him to stop at once altogether. Reduce his allowance every day for three or four days and then tell him positively he does not care to drink anymore! Then stress how proud he is that he has kicked his drinking habit and how happy it has made everyone he loves. Tell him what a credit he will be to his family, friends and all those for and with whom he works. Spread a bright future before him as a nondrinker and appeal to his pride and ambition. Use this method when working with any client who wants to master his drinking habit.

MASTERING THE HABIT OF TAKING DRUGS (MARIJUANA, COCAINE & HEROIN)

Deeply hypnotize the client who wishes to stop drugs and directly suggest:

"When I awaken you from deep hypnosis, you will say NO to drugs forever. All dangerous drugs such as marijuana, cocaine and heroin you will positively abhor. All craving is

completely gone. It is easy for you to stop the habit of taking any kind of vicious drugs and you are so proud you have."

Repeat these suggestions over and over to the hypnotized person. His attitude towards taking drugs will drastically alter. Sometimes the habit becomes mastered immediately. With other suggestions, a gradual cutting down until there is no more habit left works best. As a hypnotherapist, you must use your intuition as to how best to handle things.

MASTERING THE SMOKING HABIT

Hypnotize the client and tell him that he hates the smell of tobacco smoke and he cannot smoke tobacco anymore. He positively detests cigarettes and will decrease the number of cigarettes that he smokes each day. Less and less, until he smokes no more at all. Picture a bright future for him as a nonsmoker now and, on the last treatment, tell him definitely that when he tries to smoke a cigarette, it will taste like rubber in his mouth and will actually make him sick. Awaken him from trance and hand him a cigarette and ask him to smoke it. If he does and it makes him deadly ill and he tosses it away in nauseous disdain, you will know that he is cured. Three or four such treatments are sufficient to cure the worst cigarette smoker. The cure applies to all forms of tobacco habits.

MASTERING THE STUTTERING HABIT

This is a habit no medicine on earth will help, yet it can be effectively corrected by hypnotism. Exactly how long it will take to cure a case of stuttering is hard to say. It depends on how deeply the habit is ingrained in the speech behavior patterns of the person. To cure a stammerer requires tact and patience on the part of the hypnotherapist. However, some wonderful cures have been accomplished via hypnotic suggestions. Possibly, the handling of an actual case will best present the modus operandi:

The stutterer was a young man of seventeen. He stammered badly. It seems that his father had been a stutterer, as was also his grandfather. Stuttering seemed to have been pretty much a family affair. In the prehypnosis interview, many questions were asked to ascertain the words and letters he had most difficulty pronouncing. He had a great difficulty in saying the following letters when the words commenced with them: letters B, D, G, F, L, W and Y. He also could not answer the telephone.

Following this interview of his condition, he was hypnotized. It was suggested that he open his eyes without awakening from the trance and conversation was started with him about everyday affairs. Care was taken to note the words particularly difficult for him to pronounce. He was then directed to repeat such words over and over until he spoke them fluently. He was then given a newspaper to read and at every word he hesitated until it was suggested that he repeat it until it was perfectly pronounced. Then a book was given to him to read and the same speech hesitation corrected until he spoke perfectly. Under hypnosis he improved remarkably.

Then it was directly suggested to his subconscious:

"From now on you will have no more trouble in pronouncing the letters B and D. You will speak them fluently. You can speak and read perfectly well. When you awaken from hypnosis, you will continue to relax and experience an inner calmness so that you can read and speak with ease. You will be relaxed and at ease at all times. You will feel confident when you answer the

114

telephone and speak into it with freedom. You will have no further trouble in speaking from now on."

These suggestions were repeated to the hypnotized client a dozen times before arousing him from the trance state.

The following day, another hypnotic session was conducted working on the letters G and F, and so on. In working with a stutterer, the hypnotherapist should be precise and take time not to rush the case or give too many suggestions at the same time. Daily treatments were given and finally perfect speech was obtained. The stutterer no longer stuttered.

ALL HABITS CAN BE CURED BY HYPNOSIS

As habits are seated in the subconscious, hypnosis provides the perfect therapy. Drug habits, worry, melancholia, phobias and neurosis all yield to hypnotic suggestion. The list of habits that can be corrected goes on and on: kleptomania, lying, bragging, perversion, nervous difficulties, bedwetting, swearing, gambling, bashfulness, stubbornness, etc.. All these and more are readily cured through hypnotherapy. The untold benefits are almost beyond comprehension, as long as the client truly desires to be cured. Desire causes the "will" to act and, if the latter is properly directed, nothing can resist the influence.

CHAPTER TWENTY-TWO

THE ART OF MAGNETIC HEALING

Some people seem to be just natural healers. Often they are not even well educated persons or ones who have the slightest idea of how they affect cures, but somehow just their "laying on of hands" seems to heal persons whom they touch. It is Magnetic Healing and it seems almost to work like magic.

While some people just seem to naturally have this healing talent, it is a magic that can be developed by all who try, as it is a healing power that resides in everyone.

In this text, there is no need to go deeply into causes, as effects are what we seek. Suffice to say, there is a force with the human being, akin to a current of electricity, that can be used to heal the sick. Some call it "Animal Magnetism" or a "Magnetic Fluid" which emanates from the healthy person and transfers itself to the sick body by the force of will of the healer. Somehow it seems to stimulate, regenerate and balance the functions of the body, replacing ill-being with well-being. In Chapter Twenty of this book, instructions were given for using hypnotic suggestion in the treatment of various diseases. In this chapter, you will be instructed in how to use your personal magnetism for curing the same diseases.

LESSON ONE

The first essential of Magnetic Healing is unlimited confidence in your ability to perform a cure. Confidence in yourself inspires confidence in others. If you are able to inspire confidence of the healing from your treatment by the client, he is half way cured already. To illustrate:

Suppose you go to a physician and tell him your troubles and he tells you positively that the medicine he gives you will cure you in a day or so. His very manner of self-confidence that he can help you makes you feel better already. On the other hand, if the doctor seems uncertain as to what your ailment is and what to prescribe for it, he has not inspired confidence and will, nine times out of ten, do you little good.

So when you use the technique of Magnetic Healing, cultivate a confident air and know exactly what you are doing. Learn your lessons well and go about your work in a businesslike manner. Do not try to convince people that you can cure them against their will. Above all, never lose your temper! Never get into an argument with a client over your Magnetic Healing methods. If he should say he does not believe in your form of therapy, simply tell him, "Belief is not necessary for a cure," and if he will allow you to try to help him, he will soon be convinced of the curative power of your treatment. Play it cool.

If your client is taking medicine of some kind which his physician has prescribed , do not tell him to desist from taking that medicine. That is the physician's business, not yours. Always cooperate with the physician. Your treatment is an adjunct to help.

The Art of Magnetic Healing can produce such wonderful results as to seem almost incredible to the uninformed, but when it is remembered that the science is as old as the hills and the "laying on of hands" was used by Christ in the performance of His healing work, we must concede there is a great deal to it. Christ did not claim the power to heal was His alone. He taught His disciples and told them to go forth and relieve the suffering of mankind. They went forth, did as the Master told them, and many of the sick were healed.

It does not matter to a sick person how he is cured as long as he is made well, i.e., it is immaterial to the sufferer what means are taken to accomplish it so long as the healing is accomplished. So we are now ready to proceed on to Lesson Two.

LESSON TWO

Magnetic Healing is mainly accomplished by passes and suggestions. Some will say that suggestion is not a part of it. But as a hypnotherapist you know full well it is. It is wisest to delve into both the psychological as well as the physiological aspects of Magnetic Healing in mastering the art to produce a cure. The passes, by means of which the healing body energy (or animal magnetism) is thrown into the body of the client, are suggestions in themselves. Every movement the operator makes when giving treatments is suggestion in operation, as is your firm conviction you can cure him is your own mental suggestion that you can affect a cure. If your willpower is strong and you concentrate upon it as the purpose of the work in hand and, plainly speaking, MAKE UP YOUR MIND to cure him, you are sending a powerful suggestion to the brain of the client telepathically and it will have its effect. On the reverse, if you perform your Magnetic Healing actions mechanically and your mind is wandering from the purpose of the treatment while making passes over the person to be healed, the results will be but meager. So make this your rule when you perform Magnetic Healing in giving treatments: Keep your attention on the operation and put your heart and soul into your work. The results will be astonishing.

In such treatments, always remember that the will forces the Magnetism from your body wherever it is desired and regenerates the diseased part of your client.

So be sure to use your willpower and keep your mind on what you are doing. Do not let it wander. To facilitate concentration of your will and to induce a receptive condition in the client, always perform the treatment in a quiet room and be alone with the person you are healing (except for close relatives or friends). Other persons in the room will only prove a distraction.

Have the ill person take a seat in a chair, or if very ill, lie upon a couch or bed. Have him take a comfortable position so he can relax all his muscles as much as he can and have him close his eyes. He is not to open his eyes again until you give him permission to do so. It is important to the treatment that he should not open his eyes until the treatment is completed. Insist on this point strongly. Now, some other points to bear in mind:

Hot breath is very beneficial in any case where pain exists. Instructions will be given how to use it later in these directions. Passes over the body of the ill person are always made in a downward fashion, i.e. from head down toward the feet. The general rule is to start a pass about eight to ten inches above the seat of pain and draw your hands downward over the affected part throwing in your energy as you make the pass and flip it off your fingertips as you conclude the making of the long pass. In making healing passes, use both hands when possible and spread the fingers slightly. Make the passes with an even stroking motion, not too fast and not too slow. As you make these passes, you will experience a tingling electric-like current flowing out of your fingertips into the body of your client. It is a distinct sensation. It is a very rare, tangible force and the more you use it, the more powerful it will become. As the energy flows out of your hands, concentrate your thoughts of curing and project them along with the force into the body of the client at the point where healing is needed.

There is no set time for the special treating of any ailment. Some will have an immediate cure, while others may take several sessions or possibly even longer. But the moral is: NEVER GIVE UP.

LESSON THREE

You will now be given specific instructions for treating each disease or trouble via the Magnetic Healing process. Familiarize yourself with the foregoing and right here and now come to appreciate the value of magnetized water. As you have learned, in this form of treatment a certain force of healing energy actually passes from the operator to the client and invigorates and regenerates him by exterior manipulation and mental influence. Magnetized water makes it possible to introduce this force internally. It will prove very good medicine indeed, so in performing this kind of healing, have the person drink a glass of magnetized water before commencing external operations. Here is how to magnetize a glass of water:

Take a glass of fresh water of normal temperature (not iced) and set it on your left hand, closing the hand around it as much as possible while resting the hand and glass upon a table.

Now, using your right hand, press the thumb against the first three fingers in the manner of taking a pinch of salt, and hold the hand in this position over the glass to within an eighth of an inch above the surface of the water in the glass. Now, will with all your power that the force of Magnetism shall pass into the water. Hold the hand in this manner and perform this operation for about five minutes.

So prepared, have the ill person drink the water slowly and while you are watching him drink it, mentally will it to invigorate him and help you affect a cure. Magnetized water usually gets crystal clear like water from a spring. In magnetizing the water, never hold your left hand over the glass, unless you are left handed. If you are naturally right-

120

handed, consider your right hand as being your positive pole and your left hand the negative. If you should try to magnetize the water with your left hand, it will get flat and stale and will have a queer taste. It will then act negative instead of positive upon the person drinking it.

Here is an experiment you can try: Take two glasses of water filled to the brim and place the palms of your hands over each so as to exclude all air for five minutes. Then remove your hands and taste the water in each glass. You will find that the water in the glass which has become lukewarm has a flat taste, while the water in the other glass is sparkling and fresh, invigorating to drink.

Always give a person a glass of magnetized water to drink before actual treatment if possible, and impress on their mind its internal value to their healing.

As a Magnetic Healer, never perform any work with clients other than at times when you are feeling in good health and top shape.

LESSON FOUR

Be sure to familiarize yourself with the previous lessons thoroughly so you can perform all the processes precisely and with full confidence. Some almost miraculous cures are often produced.

Now, here is the modus operandi for using Magnetic Healing in treating various diseases. These are similar to those given in Chapter Twenty using Suggestive Therapeutics as the method. Here is the handling for curing such using the process of Magnetic Healing.

FOR HEADACHE

Seat the client in a chair with a low back, so the person's head is free for you to work on. Magnetize a glass of water and have him slowly drink it. Then ask him to relax his muscles and sit comfortably as possible with his hands lying on his thighs. Tell him to close his eyes. Ask him not to open them until you are through with the treatment and give him permission to open them. If the headache is in his forehead, place your left hand firmly across the back of his head near the base of the brain and your right hand across his forehead. In this hand-clasp, press in on the head firmly in an upward direction. Hold this pressure for a full minute. Then stand behind the person and using both your hands, make passes from the center of the forehead over the temples. At the end of each pass, throw off the collected energy. "Throw off" means to fling or snap your hands outward in such manner as if you had some sticky substance you wanted to free from your fingers, as though you had drops of honey on your fingertips and desired to shake them off. One fling at the end of each pass is sufficient. This "throwing off" applies to all cases where you use passes. It is a disposing of old and unwanted force so your hands are clear to bring in the fresh and new.

To continue removing the headache, after you have made passes for about three minutes, use the pressure again. Then make further passes for a couple of minutes more, as described. Then stand behind the person and tell them to inhale a deep breath through the nose and exhale it through the mouth. Perform this breathing about four times.

While he is thus breathing in and out, will powerfully that his headache has disappeared. All pain is gone! Then using a fan of any kind, wave it up and down the heart side of his body. This makes a slight breeze. Then say to him:

"When I count to four, I want you to open your eyes and you will find that your headache is gone and you feel fine. One, two, three, four. Now, you are all right."

As a rule, the client will feel his head and exclaim that the pain is gone. Avoid talking further on the subject if the person feels all right. If there should be some residue of pain remaining, give another treatment at once. The time for headache removal treatment should not exceed ten minutes.

Further to this Magnetic Healing treatment: All the while you are giving the treatment, use your willpower and concentrate your thoughts, willing that the headache should leave. The same applies to all other cases with which you work. Think always of what you are doing and concentrate your mind upon it. If the headache is on top of the head, press same as before, but make passes down the side of the head. If the pain is in the back of the head, make passes down the back of the head to the shoulders and throw off. Then proceed as instructed.

If the client is a woman, have her take down her hair so you can work closer to the scalp. Headaches respond readily to the treatment and provide good first experience for you in working with Magnetic Healing. Once you have learned how to relieve a headache, you will be able to relieve most any kind of pain.

Sometimes when making passes over the head while directing the magnetic energy, the client will almost fall asleep. If this should happen, simply clap your hands close to his ear and say:

"All right! Your headache is gone. Wake up!"

Make a few upward passes without touching the person, starting from the waist up to and over the head, which will dispel any sleepiness.

It is always well to tell a person to drink more water, as that is a great help in cleansing the body of any disease. Tell him to drink it slowly, not at one gulp, but to sip it while thinking of it bringing good health into his body. Have him do this regularly.

FOR TOOTHACHE

This method of using the breath upon a cloth pad was suggested as a means of removing a headache in Chapter Twenty under Suggestive Therapeutics. It is here adapted for use in removing a toothache.

Have the client sit comfortably. Give him a glass of magnetized water to drink slowly. Then tell him to close his eyes. Find out the location of the tooth that aches and you are ready to remove the pain.

Make passes where the bad tooth is located in the jaw downward along the side of the jawbone and throw off. Make about a dozen of these passes. Then take a cloth pocket handkerchief (never use a silk cloth), fold it into a pad and place it over the spot where the aching tooth is. Then blow your hot breath in the center of the cloth pad as it rests upon the cheek. In blowing hot breath filled with magnetism, do this:

Inhale through the nose and exhale through the mouth slowly. It produces a warm current of air. Place your lips on the cloth and force the breath through the cloth. It produces a warmth upon the cheek which passes the magnetic influence through the cheek and it will reach the tooth or seat of pain. Inhale and exhale the warm breath upon the cloth ten times, then remove the cloth pad. Make passes for a minute or two over the painful spot, use hot breath again, then verbalize these suggestions:

"When I count four, open your eyes and you will feel the toothache is gone and you are feeling fine. One, two, three, FOUR. Now, you are all right."

You will find that hot breath blown into a folded handkerchief pad will be helpful to use in removing all types of pain in special spots upon the body. The breath is an excellent conveyor of healing energy.

FOR ARTHRITIS

This is the Magnetic Healing way of helping arthritic and rheumatic related maladies.

Seat the person or have him lie on a bed, all depending on where the seat of the trouble is located. Give him a glass of magnetized water, then proceed.

Make passes over the area of his trouble while concentrating your thoughts on the healing taking place. For instance, if the pain is in the elbow, start your passes from the shoulder down to the fingertips and throw off. Then use hot breath on the seat of pain, use passes again, then terminate with the "suggestion formula" that the pain is gone and he is healing. If the pain is in the knee, start eight or ten inches above and throw off at the toes. Be sure to instruct the person to drink a half glass of water every day. It will aid him greatly in affecting a permanent cure of this painful disease.

Keep in mind your hands must not be cold when you make the passes. Never have cold hands when giving any form of Magnetic Healing treatment. Rub them briskly for a few moments and get them warm before ever touching the skin of a patient. When possible, remove any clothing necessary to get as close to the skin as you can. Have a basin of warm water nearby and whenever you finish a pass, dip your fingers into it after you throw off the force, leaving them wet before making another pass. This treatment for rheumatic type disorders should be frequently performed until the swelling is reduced.

FOR NEURALGIA

Generally speaking, use the same method as applied to headaches.

FOR EARACHE

Place folded cloth pad over ear and blow hot breath. Make passes over the ear and around it and draw off at the shoulder point. Always have the person take a few deep breaths at the conclusion of the treatment.

FOR HEART TROUBLE

Hypnotize client and blow hot breath over the heart. Make passes over the heart and draw off to left side of body. Make the passes over the heart for a full ten minutes. Follow the general directions you have learned for treatment and treat every other day.

FOR GENERAL DISABILITY

Have the client lie on his stomach and make passes from the crown of the head down the full length of the spine, then draw the hands across the kidneys and down along each leg to the toes and draw off. Make passes for ten minutes and increase the speed of them gradually. Use no hot breath in working with this disease. Turn the client over on his back and make passes from the shoulders down, first over the body to the toes, then over the arms to the fingertips. Then shake off fully. Perform this treatment for ten minutes at each session, which is best when given to the client when they are in bed and ready to go to sleep. After treatment, let sleep come naturally. The following morning, the client will be much improved.

FOR EYE TROUBLE

Blow hot breath on the eyes and gently stroke the eyelids towards the nose for some minutes, then use hot breath again. The blowing of breath upon the cloth pad placed on the eyes is very restful to the eyes. In many instances, Magnetic Healing has improved vision.

FOR FEVER

Fever of any kind responds well to Magnetic Healing. Place your hand on the client's forehead for a few minutes, then make passes down the body to the toes and throw off. Continue this for ten or fifteen minutes. Tell him when he opens his eyes that the fever has left him and he feels much better.

FOR PARALYSIS

Use hypnotic trance in connection with working on paralysis in combination with your Magnetic Healing processes. Remove clothing if necessary to expose the paralyzed part. Make passes over the area and increase speed of passes for ten to fifteen minutes. Then slap the area until color commences to show and a better circulation of blood is produced. Suggest firmly that he will get better and better. If, for example, you have been working on a paralyzed leg, have him try to use the leg after treatment. Paralysis responds well to hypnotic suggestion.

FOR INDIGESTION

Make passes from the neck down over the chest and stomach of the client. Use hot breath and manipulate the stomach thoroughly for fifteen minutes. Instruct the client to drink plenty of water and to restrain from eating too much meat. Substitute fruit for meat. Several treatments will often bring about a permanent cure.

GENERAL INSTRUCTIONS FOR THE SUCCESSFUL PERFORMANCE OF MAGNETIC HEALING

Here are ten rules to follow:

1. Know that you can help. Be confident in your ability to heal.
2. Be cheerful in your work. Let the person know you have helped many people with conditions far worse than their own.
3. Seat the client comfortably so he can relax and start the session by giving him a glass of magnetized water to slowly drink.
4. Have the client close his eyes at the beginning of the session and do not allow him to open them until you give permission to do so at the end of the session.
5. Except for close relatives or friends, dismiss all

other people from the room when working with a client. Magnetic Healing is largely a private matter between operator and client.

6. Have your hands warm when making passes. When convenient, soak your hands in warm water for ten minutes prior to making passes over the body. Then dry your hands and shake them vigorously to get the circulation flowing strongly.

7. In the throwing off process, at the end of the passes, dip your hands in warm water for a moment before commencing another pass.

8. Become conscious of the flow of magnetic energy in your hands. Experience it fully as an electrical tingling in your fingers. When you lay a hand on an affected part, sense the energy passing into the patient from your hands. Do the same with the breath. Experience the force.

9. Develop a rapport with your client and when a cure is achieved, instruct him to tell no one. Magnetic Healing is a private affair.

10. Combine the use of Suggestive Therapeutics with Magnetic Healing. The combination is very powerful.

Never work on a contagious disease. That is not your domain. Properly used in a conscientious manner, Magnetic Healing has great value and many wonderful cures have been reported.

Finally, is it real or just imagination? Just imagination ... how do we tend to run down imagination, never fully appreciating that imagination is the creative function of the mind, and that everything created starts in the imagination? Imagination; use it fully in all forms of hypnotic work.

America's favorite hypnotist, Tom Silver, and Australia's number one
son of stage hypnosis, Martin St. James. Taipei, Taiwan, R.O.C..
July 1997

CHAPTER TWENTY-THREE

DEVELOPING YOUR PERSONAL MAGNETISM

Charisma is a synonym for personal magnetism. It is charm. It is exerting your personality to influence. In that sense, it is a form of hypnotism. It might be interpreted to mean exerting a hypnotic influence over others without arousing the least bit apprehension. People obey your commands through this mental influence. The more you develop your personal magnetism, in direct ratio, the better hypnotist you will be.

Personal magnetism has been the means of success for top ranking people. John F. Kennedy is an excellent example of personality in action. His personality influenced all of America and an entire generation. A great entertainer like Elvis Presley is another example. His personality was so powerful that all the world followed his life and career, on and off the stage. Let's boil it down to the personality of yourself.

Some people are naturally endowed with personal magnetism; others acquire it by persistent practice. One may win success in some degree without personal magnetism, but the person will never attain great heights without it in the way of living a truly successful life. Whether you are a businessman, physician, politician, actor, lawyer or salesman, it is a gift to acquire. For the hypnotist, it is the becoming of a really GREAT hypnotist.

The man or woman who has developed this mighty power need never lack friends, for everybody wants the magnetic personality. There is something irresistibly fascinating about a magnetic personality that is difficult to describe in words. It is felt, invisible-like, and compels admiration. A man may carry his magnetism in his voice. It may be carried in his eyes. Others manifest it in their gestures, smiles and self-confidence of bearing. Some will develop it in one direction and others in another, but everyone can become magnetic to a greater extent by following the instructions given you in this chapter. You can use your personal knowledge of self-hypnosis for the development of this power.

CULTIVATING SELF-CONTROL

You cannot expect to control others unless you can control yourself. Remember this. Learn to know yourself. Find your faults and correct them. Find your good qualities and amplify them. What you will learn here will help you become magnetic.

In other words, it will increase your charisma. It will increase your charm. So it can be said: the first essential for developing a magnetic personality is your personal self-control.

The second essential is confidence in yourself and in your ability to develop a magnetic personality. This is a matter of willpower. You must have the necessary willpower to carry out your desire. You must be strong and firm in the mastery of yourself. To be strong and firm does not mean you should be egotistical. An egotist is usually stubborn. Stubbornness is a sign of a weak will. A person who will not be amenable to others from pure stubbornness denies everything and is anything but strong willed.

The man with magnetic personality can always master the man who is stubborn. If you would influence such a person, never argue with him. Remember, "where ignorance is bliss, it is folly to be wise." Try to lead him with something that interests him and side with him. Play on his ego and you will accomplish your purpose. By way of an example, if you are a salesman, lead with a smile. Many an important business transaction has been successfully accomplished by a winning smile.

Cultivate the faculty of giving quick decisions and sticking to them. Do not change them until you are absolutely convinced you are wrong. A vacillating, unsteady disposition is anti-personality.

Become a master of anger within yourself. If you feel anger arousing within you, right in the middle STOP AND TAKE THREE DEEP BREATHS so that you become rational and deal with it, not allowing it to undermine your personality. Anger takes away your vitality and weakens your well-being. Conversely, cheerful thoughts are infecting, and their radiation produces corresponding actions in the minds of others. A magnetic personality radiates sunshine and good will, and these thoughts are contagious.

If you are in company and there is discussion of things on which you are not especially well informed, do not force your views. Just be a good listener. Avoid debate unless you are absolutely sure of your ground. Some people like to talk just to hear themselves talk, without really saying anything. They are a bore and boredom is anti-personality.

Some people are magnetic to some extent, but their use of language destroys their influence. Use tact and study the characteristics of the person you wish to influence. Gain confidence, for "confidence begets confidence".

All persons are magnetic to some degree and the power can definitely be developed. The basic principle of personal magnetism is strong willpower. Personal magnetism is a nerve force which is produced and directed by the will of the producer. The will can be strengthened by exercising it. You cannot expect the will to be strong without training. Hypnosis (self-hypnosis), used upon yourself provides a remarkable way to exercise the will and develop WILL-POWER.

THE TECHNIQUE OF SELF-HYPNOSIS

This technique employs the ideomotor response idea, that every thought held is the mind produces an accompanying subjective response in the body. That is to say, if we consciously think an idea, we subconsciously tend to move in that direction. This is the process you can effectively use to increase your personal magnetism.

Take a seat and THINK about yawning and actually yawn. As you do this, you will find yourself really yawning and yawning is very relaxing to the body, moving in the direction of sleep and deliberately thinking of going to sleep moves you into hypnotic sleep, wherein mind becomes activated to accept suggestions, as you know. Now, close your eyes and THINK of how you are becoming relaxed all over. THINK of how receptive your subconscious mind is becoming to accept and act upon the suggestions you are going to implant in it that will increase your personal magnetism. Continue on, relaxing, and THINK sleep. THINK GOING TO SLEEP. THINK sleep. You will find yourself becoming very sleepy, but just let your mind drift and don't allow yourself to actually go to sleep. You are close to sleep, yet still not asleep. You have placed yourself into self-hypnosis.

In this receptive and passive condition of mind, place the palms of your hands over your ears and press in a little. Now, SPEAKING OUT LOUD TO YOURSELF, present these suggestions which, by this process, will seem to "ring" inside your head:

FOR CULTIVATING SELF-CONFIDENCE

"I .. am .. a .. man (or woman, as the case may be). I .. have .. strong .. willpower. My .. will .. is .. powerful. I ..

134

believe .. in .. myself .. and .. my .. ability .. to .. succeed.
My .. personality .. is .. becoming .. magnetic .. and ..
nothing .. can .. prevent .. me .. from .. succeeding. My ..
will .. is .. strong. My .. confidence .. in .. myself .. is ..
unlimited. I .. will .. rely .. absolutely .. on .. myself. My
.. confidence .. cannot .. be .. shaken."

Repeat these suggestions to yourself in this special mental
state three times. Then, drop your hands from pressing on
your ears to relax into your lap and go to sleep, if you wish.
Awaken when you will.

These are enough self-suggestions for the first session.
The next day, you can try another. Apply the same method
to induce self-hypnosis in yourself and present to yourself
these suggestions:

FOR CULTIVATING DETERMINATION

"I .. am .. developing .. a .. magnetic .. personality. I .. am
.. determined .. to .. succeed. I .. will .. complete ..
successfully .. everything .. I .. start .. out .. to .. do. I ..
have .. the .. ability .. to .. influence .. people. People ..
respond .. to .. the .. influence .. of .. my .. personal ..
magnetism. People .. respond .. to .. the .. power .. of .. my
.. will. I .. am .. determined .. to .. radiate .. cheerfulness ..
at .. all .. times. I .. have .. powerful .. determination .. to ..
do .. whatever .. I .. set .. out .. to .. do. Nothing .. can ..
deter .. me. The .. power .. of .. self-confidence .. is .. mine.
The .. power .. of .. determination .. is .. mine .. as .. well.
It .. is .. the .. case."

Repeat these suggestions to yourself three times while in
the state of self-hypnosis you have induced, then go to sleep.
Awaken when you will. End of session for this day.

FOR CULTIVATING SELF-CONTROL

Induce the self-hypnosis state in yourself and proceed as before. With palms of hands pressing against your ears, repeat out loud these suggestions:

"I .. have .. full .. control .. of .. myself .. at .. all .. time. I .. will .. never .. lose .. my .. temper. No .. one .. can .. ruffle .. me. I .. will .. always .. have .. a .. smile .. when .. needed. I .. will .. never .. be .. discouraged. I .. will .. never .. be .. nervous. I .. am .. the .. controller. I .. am .. master .. of .. myself .. and .. master .. of .. others .. at .. all .. times. I .. do .. not .. needlessly .. worry. I .. am .. cheerful .. and .. happy. My .. WILLPOWER .. is .. vast .. and .. supreme .. and .. I .. have .. a .. magnetic .. personality .. that .. will .. influence .. others .. as .. it .. is .. my .. will .. to .. cause. My .. eyes .. exert .. this .. power. My .. entire .. BEING .. exerts .. this .. power. I .. have .. developed .. a .. MAGNETIC PERSONALITY."

Repeat three times and conclude the session the same as always. Awaken when you will. Use this process daily for a few weeks. The results will amaze you in the qualities of personal magnetism it will cultivate in your personality.

REINFORCING SELF-HYPNOTIC SUGGESTIONS

Write the suggestions you have given yourself on paper. Write each exercise on a separate sheet so you are prepared. In your private room, just before going to bed, darken the room and place a lit candle on a table before a comfortable chair in which you seat yourself. Have the candle positioned high enough so that you have to open your eyes wide in looking at the flame. Now study the paper containing one of the willpower exercises you have written. As you read its message, speak out loud to yourself what you are reading. Read it and speak it thus several times, committing it more or less to memory. Then relax in the chair, stare directly at the candle flame and as you stare at it, repeat verbally what you have memorized. When your eyes get tired, close them and relax even more. Now, mentally review what you have been speaking. Continue to do this until you can absorb no more and just want to go to sleep. Go to bed and have a good night's sleep.

Use only one setting of the willpower exercises at each of these reinforcement sessions. Sometimes, after looking at the candle flame for awhile, it will seem as if it were becoming very large and you will seem to see the suggestions written in the flame. When this illusion happens, it means your self-suggestions have very much become your own.

Personal magnetism is essential to your outstanding success as a hypnotist. Follow these instructions and develop your WILL and you will achieve your highest ambitions for success in life. Persevere, practice and you will cultivate PERSONAL MAGNETISM.

Tom Silver and Mr. Chuck Norris "International Movie and Television Star" and "Black Belt Karate and Martial Arts Expert" talking after Tom's Hypnosis Stage Show Backyard Performance in Southern California on New Year's Eve December 31st. 1999

138

CHAPTER TWENTY-FOUR

PERSONAL MAGNETISM FOR THE PROFESSIONS

Personal magnetism and hypnotism are invaluable to the various professions. No great professional success can be attained without the practical employment of this wonderful power. Its use will benefit you in every way.

FOR THE LAWYER

Every successful lawyer, pleading his case before a jury, uses hypnotic suggestion, especially criminal lawyers. The judge's and the jury's attention is skillfully drawn towards him and every ounce of will power and magnetism is directed toward them to get their minds to accept his view of the case. No lawyer can hope to attain full use of the Power of Suggestion without combining it with Personal Magnetism.

FOR THE PHYSICIAN

No profession can use the power of personal magnetism more importantly that that of the physician. In connection with his medical knowledge, the use of hypnotism and magnetism will make him paramount in his profession. In addition to being a doctor, he will become a healer. By using these processes, he will be able to affect cures that would be otherwise impossible. The physician who uses what has been instructed in this text will have gained the full confidence of his patients for his ability to make them well. Therein lies a great secret for the healing of the sick.

FOR THE MINISTER

The minister has a wonderful opportunity to use the power of suggestion and personal magnetism. The minister who has personal magnetism is the one who fills his church. Such a minister knows how to keep and attract the attention of the congregation. He is magnetic. He emanates forceful and powerful thought waves each time he delivers a sermon. His personal magnetism attracts people to his pews like bits of iron are attracted to a magnet.

FOR THE SALESMAN

The most far sweeping field for the use of personal magnetism and hypnotic influence is in the profession of salesmanship. The "knight of the grip", the insurance solicitor, the canvasser, the clerk behind the counter, the merchandise salesman, the real estate broker, everyone connected with the profession of salesmanship, the list goes on and on, could easily double their sales by the use of hypnotic suggestion combined with his cultivated personal magnetism. All persons engaged in the business of selling to the public would do well to study this text thoroughly and master what it tells.

SELF-HYPNOSIS FOR THE USE OF ALL PROFESSIONS

As you have learned the technique of self-hypnosis, let each professional design his own suggestion-formulae which apply especially to his work. Then put such formulae into operation exactly as has been described in the obtaining of personal magnetism for the individual. A bit of thought, a little effort, and the professional results achieved are excellent.

CHAPTER TWENTY-FIVE

SELF HYPNOSIS FOR PERSONAL USE

SELF-INDUCED ANESTHESIA

All people have the power to render their own body immune to pain, but few of them have ever mastered this gift. Some persons seem to develop this power spontaneously, but most have need to practice. Self-confidence, willpower, concentration of direct thought and patient practice are required. Some children have been able to acquire this power as part of their nature. Such a child can be spanked severely and yet feels nothing in the way of pain.

Stage hypnotists are frequently seen to pass a needle through a subject's cheek or the flesh of the arm, and no pain at all is experienced as a result of the anesthetic suggestions given prior to the penetration. Stories are often told of how the fakirs of India pass pins through most any part of their body without experiencing the slightest discomfort.

Developing the ability to establish anesthesia takes practice, but you can acquire it if you wish. Use the same general technique of inducing hypnosis in yourself that you have learned and direct into your mind, in precisely the same way, suggestions for the abolishment of pain sensations. It will seem startling, even to yourself, the results that are obtained with surprisingly little practice in that direction.

The mastering of pain, i.e. producing self-induced anesthesia is but the beginning of the remarkable things you can do to benefit yourself using this power.

Whatever you have learned to do for others when you hypnotize them, you can equally do for yourself when you hypnotize yourself.

HYPNOTIC INFLUENCE FOR SUPER-LEARNING

The use of hypnotism for increasing learning ability is outstanding. Most learning is largely a matter of retaining the information taught and recalling it readily when it is required. The subconscious mind operates like the memory banks of a computer and all information stored therein can be recalled when you press the right buttons, as it were. Self-hypnosis can give you that ability.

The night before the examination takes place, instead of staying up all night trying to cram, place yourself in a hypnotic state and give your inner mind the suggestion that all the answers will pop out and appear on your "screen of mind". Write down what appears and there you are. Learn how to do this and you will come out 100% each and every time.

When you study and when you receive instructions from a teacher, just relax and listen. Allow the information to sink in. Even taking notes is not necessary, unless one is in the habit of taking notes. Actually, the information given you is all there for the taking.

If you want to recall something you have been taught and cannot seem to recall it, just relax and stop trying so hard. Just let your mind drift, while holding onto the thought as to where you want it to drift. Answers will seem to float in all by themselves.

The secret is to make the effort to recall without trying hard to recall. In other words, make the effort without the effort.

Many examinations given these days are based on knowing whether a question asked is right or wrong and the examination requires that the student place a plus (+) for right before the question asked if it is correct and a minus (-) if it is wrong. In self-hypnosis, tell your subconscious the correct symbol will appear for each question asked in the exam. If you seem to hallucinate in seeing the symbols, so much the better. Try this and see how it comes out.

Basically it is the job of the teacher to teach and the job of the student to learn. Yet, far too often, education becomes a challenge between the teacher and the student. It is almost as though the instructors were saying, "I dare you to learn what I have to teach you." Such is the challenge and a challenge invariably sends a message of stress to the mind. Instead of a challenge, education should be presented as a game to be played and enjoyed between teacher and student. Games are fun and relaxing to the mind. Mind functions best when it is relaxed.

More and more, as the educational system begins to apply these principles of how the mind operates (many of which you have learned in this book), more and more geniuses will be produced.

"Living Room" hypnosis show with family members and friends participating in hypnotic induction where their hands and faces become the "objects of concentration" allowing them to enter into hypnosis.
1992

CHAPTER TWENTY-SIX

MORE FOR YOUR HYPNOTIC "KNOW-HOW"

HYPNOTISM IS SAFE AND SANE

The hue and cry occasionally set up by ill informed people that hypnotism is harmful to the mind is ridiculous. Hypnosis is a perfectly natural function of the mind. Millions of cases of hypnotism have been conducted all over the world and not a single, harmful result has been reported.

However, everything has both a positive and a negative aspect. The mind can take on harmful suggestions just as well as it can helpful ones. As an example, look at how Hitler hypnotized the whole nation of Germany. But by and large, hypnotists are highly principled people who are out to help humanity, not harm it. In stage demonstrations of hypnotism, the entire audience is there to witness that no harmful suggestions are presented. Furthermore, in hypnotherapy, usually a third party is present to witness the procedure with the client.

Hypnotism can be looked upon as a rapid way of changing the mind. It is an effective way to produce both physical and mental changes in the body and mind of the hypnotized individual. Mind affects body and body affects mind. Correctly used, hypnosis provides a wonderful tool for mental training. If there is ever any harm, it is never from the hypnosis. Any harm must rest entirely on the scruples of the hypnotist. However, it can equally be said that the physician is in the same boat, in relation to standards.

HYPNOTIC INFLUENCE AND CRIME

A study of hypnotic suggestion may offer some useful ideas to the penal code that are worthy of thought. Everybody is influenced, to a greater or lesser degree, by someone or something, consciously or subconsciously, by the environment to which they are exposed. Environment greatly enhances suggestive influence. If a man is continuously exposed to a criminal side of life and commences to feel that such is the best way to get along, he is likely to become a criminal. On the other hand, if he lives in an environment that goes along with the accepted protocol of society, he is most likely to so conform. He becomes a good citizen.

Beyond question, there are some persons that seem to have rebellious, antisocial instincts in them that lead to criminal behavior. However, even in such persons, there seems to be a countering trait of goodness that can often be developed. For example, as has often happened if a criminal is placed in the company of, shall we say, sensible and honest people who seem to be getting along okay in life, he will often revert to ways of good behavior rather than bad behavior for, basically, good in humanity predominates over bad. If such a man is removed from the environment of criminality and placed in an environment of usefulness to his fellow man, often a remarkable shift in attitude will occur. On the other hand, if he is sent to jail on his first offense and placed among others far more criminally minded than himself, he is very likely to sink yet deeper into attitudes of crime. In this is seen the obvious operation of hypnotic suggestion which we have learned so well, which operates so powerfully within the mind of the individual.

By removing him from the criminal influence so often found in the penitentiary and placing him in a different environment, his mentality will, hopefully, head towards reform for the better.

Physical punishment will never reform a criminal; on the contrary, it fills his mind with hatred and malice towards mankind, and at the first chance he gets, he seeks to avenge himself. On the other hand, if the appeal is made to the subliminal self via the hypnotic suggestions and example, the spark of good that is within him may be kindled.

As was mentioned, in actual experience, good seems to predominate over bad in most people. For example, a good man, even when deeply hypnotized, will not obey a suggestion against his ingrained moral nature. The instinct of self-preservation steps in and says, "No." In the same manner, a moral woman cannot be induced to perform an immoral act, and if such is insisted upon by the operator, will awaken from the hypnosis, frequently with a shock.

A dramatic experiment to induce criminal behavior in hypnotized individuals was tried in a psychological laboratories, in which a deeply hypnotized person was told that his worse enemy was before him and the suggestion made that he would kill him. The subject was then handed a length of paper suggested to be a knife and told to stab his enemy in the back. Invariably, the subject would plunge the imaginary knife in the back of his enemy. But when the same subject was handed a real knife and told to kill the enemy, the suggestion was never carried out. Some would drop the knife. Others would tremble violently when the suggestion was insisted upon. Most subjects would simply awaken immediately from the hypnosis spontaneously of their own volition.

A rule of thumb in relation to hypnotic suggestions is that the subject will carry out all suggestions given by the operator providing they do not conflict with his moral nature, personal characteristics, or produce serious consequences to himself. In a nutshell, it can be said that the subconscious mind of a person is basically protective of the individual.

AUTOMATIC WRITING AND DRAWING

Often the production of such phenomena is ascribed to influence from outside entities or spirits manifesting through the subject. Whether this is so or not is hard to say, and only an objective consideration of what comes through can give any accurate evaluation of such matters. However, there is a rule in science termed "The Law of Parsimony" which explains that, without objective evidence to the contrary, the simpler explanation is the one most likely to be the most correct. Such seems to be the case with most experiences with automatic writing, i.e. such being but an objective way for subconscious impressions to come through in the form of written messages.

It is generally conceded that the subconscious phase of mind has control over the body of the person, so it is reasonable to suppose that the control of the movements of the hands to write messages can come through independent of the conscious knowledge of the person.

There have even been reported cases in which automatic, subconscious drawings of pictures have been recorded. Some of these drawings are really wonderful examples of artwork, normally far beyond the conscious efforts of the subject. However, again, who really knows what remarkable talents lie within the subconscious minds of some persons? It is not uncommon even to hear great artists who consciously paint say that the inspiration for their painting came from out of their subconscious.

Whatever explanation one accepts as to the basic cause of automatic writing and drawing is truly irrelevant. What can be said as truth is that the subconscious mind of man is a treasure chest of wonders. Equally, it can be a Pandora's Box.

Volunteers Hypnotized by Tom Silver at
National Sports Event and Transformed into the
World's Greatest Hula Dancers "Dancing The Hula" while
Twenty-Five Thousand Fans Watch!

Ormond McGill, "Dean of American Hypnotists," performing a
hypnosis stage show in early 1970's.

151

CHAPTER TWENTY-SEVEN

ENTERTAINING WITH HYPNOTISM

There are some who frown on the performance of hypnotism as entertainment. But why? It causes no harm to anyone to perform fun things upon the stage for the enjoyment of the audience who watch. In fact, it is good for one to let one's hair down once in awhile and get free from inhibitions. The hypnotism show provides that freedom.

Indeed, when Charcot died and the Nancy School closed in France, it was stage hypnotists who kept public interest alive in the subject. Truly, the witnessing of a hypnotism show has inspired many a person to seek help from this wonderful power of the mind.

Any criticism of hypnotism as entertainment must come from what kind of entertainment is designed by the performer (but that is true of any kind of show) and not from any criticism of the phenomena observed itself. When presented in good taste, the hypnotism show provides an excellent opportunity to explain what useful help can be obtained from the intelligent use of hypnosis in the field of hypnotherapy.

ILLUSIONS AND HALLUCINATIONS

For a start on entertaining with hypnotism, it is well to understand the nature of illusions and hallucinations while the person is hypnotized. There is a wide difference between an illusion and a hallucination. By way of illustration: if you give a subject a cane and tell him it is a harmless snake, that is an illusion, but if his hand is empty and you suggest that he has a snake in it and he sees one, that is a hallucination. The latter requires more profound trance production. It is easier to tell a subject that the floor in front of him is a stream of water and have him accept the idea and react accordingly than it is to tell him that an elephant is in the room, that is unless a large piece of furniture is suggested to be the elephant.

This understanding of illusions and hallucinations should be well appreciated by the hypnotist who would entertain with this interesting science/art that people enjoy witnessing so much. Why this enjoyment? Nothing is more entertaining than "human interest" itself. The hypnotic show is directly founded on human interest. It is well for the student of hypnotism to remember the following rules when trying to create illusions or hallucinations:

1. Have the suggestions pertaining to the experiment well in mind before imparting them to the subject.
2. Give the suggestions at least three times before telling the subject to open his eyes. Repetition reinforces the suggestions and further prepares his mind to create a mental picture beforehand.
3. Give your suggestions in a positive manner and directly to the point. For example, never say, "I wish you to see." Simply say, "You will see, etc.." The subconscious mind functions best when suggestions are kept simple.
4. The moment the subject opens his eyes to see what is suggested, take your hand and point towards the imaginary object, as though you see it too. Insist that it is there.

If these four rules are adhered to, very entertaining results will be obtained. Here are some fun things that can be tried when entertaining with hypnotism:

GOIN' FISHIN'

Have the subject seated and induce as deep a depth of hypnosis as proves possible. Stand to his right and lay your left hand on the top of his head with your thumb resting at the root of his nose. Then suggest:

> "When ... I ... tell ... you ... to ... open. .. your. .. eyes, .. you. .. will ... not ... awaken, ... but ... you ... will ... find ... that ... you ... are ... sitting ... on ...the ... edge ... of ... a ... river (or lake) ... and ... you ... are ... goin' ... fishin'. The fish ... are ... biting ... and ... you ... will ... catch ... many. You ... will ... find .. a .. fishing pole ... by ... your side .. and ... you ... will ... bait ... the ... hook ... and ... fish."

Repeat three times. Then, give him a broomstick for the fish pole. Now, press slightly upwards with your thumb and say:

> "All .. right, .. open .. your .. eyes. (Quickly, say:) See .. the .. water. Look .. at .. the .. fish .. in .. there. Catch .. them."

Point towards the floor before him when telling him to see the water. After he has fished for awhile, awaken him. If you wish, you can awaken the subject between each scene, but it is not essential. You can lead him from one experiment to another by simply suggesting that the illusion has disappeared and suggesting something else, without awakening him. However, often the funniest part of the entertainment comes in awakening the subject who, when regaining consciousness, finds himself in a ludicrous situation and does not remember the performance.

Members of the "Lions Club" hypnotized by Tom Silver at the "Lions Club" International Conference Meetings in Southern California in 1985. They were all hypnotized to think that they were petting their favorite little birds that they brought to class to share with all the students in their third grade classroom!

WORLD'S GREATEST PIANO PLAYERS

Hypnotize a group of subjects and suggest to them that when you count to three, they will sit up in their chairs and hold their hands out in front of them, and play the piano, because they are the world's greatest piano players and they are playing the piano and performing at Carnegie Hall. Tell them that they will hit every note on the keyboard . Then suggest:

"When...I...count...to...three...you...are...the...world's... greatest...piano...player...and...you....are...performing... tonight...at...Carnegie...Hall...playing...the...piano. You... will...be...very.....creative....and...hit...every....note...on... the...keyboard...because...you...are...a...great...piano..player. The...world's...greatest...piano...player. On...the...count... of...three....you...are...playing...the...piano....One...Two... Three...Play...the...piano..

When performing this very visual demonstration, use real piano recorded music. As the subjects hear the music, they will become more creative and it will appear as if they are really playing the piano. You can go up to each person and comment on how well they play the piano. "Look how seriously he is playing", "See how he/she hits every note on the keyboard", "See how he/she plays with so much excitement" "Look how serious he/she is" and so forth.

ORCHESTRA CONDUCTORS

Tell your hypnotized subject or subjects that they are a great orchestra conductor and that they are conducting a large orchestra. Tell them that when you count to three, or when they hear the sound of the orchestra, they will instantly stand up and move there hands up and down and conduct the orchestra, because they are the greatest orchestra conductors in the world.

Then, say:

> "You.. are.. a... great ....orchestra.. conductor.. and.. you... are.. here.. today... to...conduct... the... Los Angeles.. Philharmonic ...Orchestra. ...and... when ...I... count... to.. three.... you... will ..stand... up... and move ...your.. hands up.. and... down ..and.. conduct... the... orchestra... because you.. are.. the... worlds greatest ...orchestra.. conductor. .. One.. Two .. Three ... Stand up!... Conduct...the... orchestra!" You...are...a...orchestra...conductor..."

On this fun hypnosis routine, you can use a counting method of one, two, three, or you can say to the subject that when they hear the orchestra playing, they will instantly stand up and conduct the orchestra.

With this method, the music starts the routine and not the counting of three. Music acts as a wonderful post-hypnotic suggestion to start a routine such as conducting an orchestra.

WATCHING A FUNNY MOVIE AND A SAD MOVIE

Hypnotize a person and say to the subject while they are hypnotized that when you count up to three, they will be watching the funniest movie that they have ever seen in their life and they will laugh out loud hysterically.

After a few moments have outrageous laughter, tell the subject that when you count to three, the movie will become the very saddest movie they have ever seen.

157

Then give the suggestion:

*"When...I...count...to...three,....you...are...in...a....movie...
theater....watching....the...funniest....movie...you....have...
ever...seen.. laughing...out...loud...because...it...is...the....
funniest...movie...that...you...have...ever...seen...in...your...
entire...life...laughing...out...loud...And...every...time....I
touch...you...on...your...forehead...the...movie...becomes...
ten...times...more...funnier....now...One...Two....Three!...
Watching a Funny Movie...Laughing.. out.. loud."*

After a few moments now say to the subject:

*"On...the...count...of...three...the...movie...is...now...a...
sad...movie...so...sad...that...you...want...to...cry...because...
the...movie...is...so...sad...On...the...count...of...three...you
are...watching...a...sad....sad...movie...One...Two...Three..
You...are...watching...the...saddest...movie...that...you...
have...ever...seen...you...are...watching..a...sad...movie.*

It is amazing to see a person instantly go from laughing to crying and back to laughing in the split of an eye. The changes on your subjects will amaze you and everyone who witnesses this marvelous demonstration. Actors would love to have this subconscious ability and talent. With hypnosis, it happens automatically.

HAWAIIAN HULA DANCERS DANCING A HULA

Hypnotize a group of subjects and tell them that they are the best hula dancers in Hawaii and that they are dancing the hula for thousands of tourists on the island. And when you count to three, or when they hear the hula music, they will stand up, move their arms around, and dance the hula.

Then give this suggestion:

"You...are...on...a...jet...plane...heading...for...Hawaii...
to...forget...all...about...your...cares...and...worries.
You...are...going...to...Hawaii...for...a...wonderful...
vacation...You...can...almost...smell...the...coconuts...
and...pineapples...and...see...the...ocean...and…waves
And...now...the...plane...has...landed...in...Hawaii...
and...on...the...count...of...three...you...will...stand...up
and...dance...the...hula...because...you...are...the...best
hula...dancers...in...Hawaii…okay...One...Two...Three
stand up....dance...the...hula...you...are…the...best…
dancers...in...Hawaii....hula...hands...and...hula
hips....swaying...to...the...music..."

While the subjects are doing the hula, you can suggest to them while they are dancing that when you count to three their left foot is stuck on the floor while they are dancing and then say, One, Two Three out loud and watch the fun and they continue to dance with one foot stuck on the ground. After the hula dancing, ask the subjects to sit back down in their chairs and close their eyes and go back into hypnotic sleep. Always remove the suggestion you have just given before you go on to your next suggestion or demonstration by saying " And now the suggestion is gone. You are no longer a hula dancer (or whatever the suggestions might be)."

PETTING A LITTLE PET BIRD IN THE THIRD GRADE

This hypnosis routine for entertainment is fun, because it brings out the little kid which is inside each and everyone of us. The suggestion is that the hypnotized subject is in the third grade and that they have brought there pet bird to school to share with all the students in the class.

The suggestion to pet their little bird goes like this:

"You...are...now...going....back....in...time...back...to... the...third..grade...you...are...in...the...third...grade and...you...have...brought...your...pet...bird...to...class to...share...with...all...the...students...and...you...have a...beautiful...bird...and...when...I...count...to...three... you...will...lift...up...your...first...finger...of...your... left...hand...and...you...be...petting...your...favorite bird... in...the...third...grade..on...the...count...of... three...petting...your...favorite...bird....in...the...third... grade...now...one....two...three....hold...your....finger out...petting...your...pet...bird...and...talk...to...your... bird....that's...a... pretty...bird....Pet...your....bird..."

During this performance of the materialization of a bird on a finger, you can go up to the subjects and ask them questions about their bird. What's the name of your bird? Tell the boys and girls what color is your bird? How long have you owned this bird? Speak to your bird? Give your little birdie a kiss? and so fourth....

MIND READER FROM INDIA

Select a person from your group of hypnotized subjects and tell him that he is a mind reader from India. He is Omar from India, and that he can read "people's minds". He has left his 1(800) number to be here at the event tonight. He will look into a person in the audience's eyes, and tell the audience or committee what that person is thinking.

Now pick a hypnotized person, touch him/her on their arm or shoulder, and give the following post hypnotic suggestion:

160

"The...person...I...am...now...touching...I...will...now...
give...you...a...post...hypnotic...suggestion....which...you...
will...respond...to...when...you...awaken...In...a...moment,.
I...will...awaken...you...out...of...hypnosis...when...I..count
up...from...1...to...3...or...When...you...hear..me...say...the.
words,....Mind...Reader..,you...will...stand...up...and...
come....forward...because,...you...are...Omar...from...India,..
a... famous... mind ...reader....You...are....here...to...read
people's...minds...You...are...Omar...from....India,...and...
you ...speak ...with ...an... Indian...Accent...You... are...
here...to...read...peoples...minds...and...tell...us...what..
they...are....thinking...Nod...your...head..."yes"...if...you
understand...me?...Good,...Okay...then,...now...one...two..
three...open...your...eyes,...wake up,... look up here..."

(Now Say to the Audience) "Ladies and gentleman, we have here tonight for your entertainment pleasure, the world's greatest **MIND READER!** Omar from India". Now look at the subject and say in a commanding voice, "Will the Mind Reader, Omar from India, please come here". Your subject, on your first command of the words, MIND READER!, will have probably already activated the suggestion of him being the Mind Reader, and he will automatically stand up and come to you. If he did not come up by hearing the words Mind Reader, then look into your subject's eyes and say, "Will the Mind Reader, Omar from India now please come here." The subject will come forward, if the suggestion has been given successfully. You then can ask the Mind Reader his name, and where is he from. Now ask the mind reader to pick a person in the audience and look into their eyes and read there mind. It's amazing to hear the stories and predictions of that Omar will create under the influence of hypnosis.

161

Hypnotist Tom Silver performing "Living Room" Hypnotism by hypnotizing a guest at a house party to think that he was The Strongest Man in the World "Superman"! December 16, 1986

TWIST DANCE CONTEST

For this demonstration, you will need some sort of sound system and a twist music dance recording.

Have a hypnotized group of people think that they have entered the "Chubby Checkers Twist Dance Contest" and that when they here the Twist Dance music, they will stand up and be competing for a ten thousand dollar prize in the twist dance contest.   Tell them that each time the music stops, they will have to stop and be in a freeze position. Each time the music stops, they "freeze" stand instantly still. Now here is your hypnotic suggestion to the hypnotized subjects seated in chairs.

"When...you...hear...the...next...music,...you...will...stand up...because...you...are...a...twist...dancer...and...you...are in...the...Chubby...Checkers...twist...dance...contest... competing...for...Ten...Thousand...Dollars!...You...are...a great...twist...dancer...and...you...want...to...win...this... contest...Whenever...you...hear...the...twist...music...stop.. you...will...instantly..."freeze"...and...stand...still,..if...you move,...you...will...be...out...of...the...contest....When...the music...starts,...you...instantly...start...dancing...When... the...music...stops,...you...freeze...and...stand...still... Now...open...you...eyes...and...awaken.

Now say to the audience, "Does everybody like music?" And right then, start the twist dance music and you will see all the subjects instantly stand up and start doing the twist. Let the music play for about 20 or so seconds, and then stop it, and they all freeze. Now start the music again and the fun just continues for as long as you like. Remember after the suggestion is over, have the subjects sit safely back down in their chairs and say "the suggestions is now gone, and you can close your eyes and go back asleep." And you are ready now to go on with your show.

Remember to always give positive suggestions to your hypnosis volunteers before you awaken them. "When you awaken out of hypnosis, the suggestions I have just given you, will be gone, but I will now leave you with some positive suggestions for you to take home with you. Tonight when you are ready for sleep, you will sleep deeply and positively. You will awaken in the morning felling great. When I count to five, you will wake up, feel great, and you will have enjoyed your creativity while under hypnosis. You will awaken feeling refreshed, with lots of energy , confident in yourself, and with a big smile on your face. Every time you smile, from now on, you will feel more happy and good about yourself. When I count to five you will wake up out of hypnosis . One, Two Three, Four, Five, now open your eyes, wake up, and smile.

STEP ON THE ANTS

The subjects think that there are ants on the ground because someone dropped some food on the floor. They will want to step on the ants, so that the ants don't crawl up there legs. This routine is not for every hypnosis show or demonstration, but it is quite visual and fun with the right group of subjects.

Hypnotize the subjects and then say to them:

On...the...count...of...three...you...will...open...your...eyes and...see...some...ants...on...the...floor...You...will...step...on these...ants,..so...that...they...do...not...crawl...up...your... legs...They...will...not...hurt...you,...but...you...do...not... want...them...to...crawl...up...your...legs....On...the..count of...three,...step...on...the...ants....One...Two...Three...Step on...the ...ants.

This stage hypnosis routine, is very visual as well as the stamping on the ground by the subjects makes for some fun noises and everybody in the audience will just crack up. When the routine is over, you can say to your subject/volunteers:

The...ants...are...gone...close...your...eyes...and...forget about...it...it...was...just...an...imagination...and...you... feel...just...fine...now...close...your...eyes...deep...asleep..

LAZY TONGUE SLIPS OUT OF YOUR MOUTH

This routine is about having the hypnotized subject think that they have a lazy tongue and that every time they try to speak, they will find their tongue just slips right out of their mouth. They can not speak because their tongue keeps getting in the way. You then awaken the subject and ask him or her questions about themselves, or ask them to read a book. After they stumble around for a while trying to speak with their lazy tongue, tell the subject that the tongue is now not lazy and that they speak simply perfectly. Now ask the subject a question, or have them read the same book. After the demonstration, turn to the audience and say, "Give this person a big applause for his wonderful concentration and creativity."
Suggest the following suggestion to the hypnotized person by saying his name, or touching his shoulder and then say the following:

"The...person...I...am...touching,...when...I...count...up...to three,...you...will...open... your...eyes...and...look...at...me. I...will...ask...you...some...questions,...or...I...will...ask... you...to...read...a...book...But...you...can't...because...each.. .and...every...time...you....open...your...mouth ...to ...speak,

your...tongue...will...slip...right...out...of...your...mouth,...
because...you...have...a...lazy...tongue...every...time...you
open...your...mouth...to...speak,...your...tongue...will...get..
lazier... and...lazier...and...slips...and...falls...right...out
of...your...mouth...You...have...a...lazy...lazy...tongue...
Slips...right...out...of...your...mouth...every...time...you...
speak... now...one, ..two,.. three, ...wake up."

Now ask the subject some questions about him or herself, or have the subject read a simple children's book and watch and hear the fun. The subject will try as hard as he can to speak, but his tongue will keep falling right out of his mouth. This routine will get you barrels of laughter from everyone, including yourself, and later on by even the subject after he realizes what had happened to him.

After the demonstration, put the subject back into hypnosis and say to him or her, "The suggestion is now gone, it was just imagination, and you speak perfect in every way. Your tongue works perfectly and you now speak and talk perfect in every way. Count up to five and wake the subject up.

SOME FUNNY STUNTS

The subject is very responsive to the hypnotist's commands. For instance, if you tell a group of subject's that they cannot speak properly but will sing their words, they will speak like they were singing, even when trying their best to speak normally. You can make them feel sad or joyful at will. Any emotion can be called forth at the hypnotist's command.

If you touch a subject's cheek and tell him he has a toothache, he will immediately howl with pain. Should he have his legs crossed and it is suggested his shoes pinch a sore corn on his foot, he will start hopping about in distress and

166

will very likely take off his shoes to examine his sore toe. Tell a subject the temperature in the room is getting awfully hot, and he will take off his coat and fan himself. Take a cane and touch the hypnotized subject while telling him it is a hot poker, and he pulls away from it mighty fast. All of these suggestions are given to the subject and/or subjects with quick, sharp commands.

An amusing experiment is to tell a subject that his coat is on wrong side out. He will quickly take it off, reverse it, and put it back on backwards. Lots of fun when you awaken him and he finds the coat reversed. A steady eye, quick decision, and unfailing willpower are all that are needed to produce these phenomena which demonstrate strikingly the power of suggestion and the magic of the mind.

Suggest to a subject that his nose is made of rubber, and he will have fun stretching it out and letting it snap back into position on his face. Tell him to make rubber balls from it and then go out among the audience and try to sell them. Tell him that he is a cat or dog and he will at once act the part of the animal suggested. He will crawl on his hands and feet and meow like a cat or bark like a dog. You can make old people believe they are children and children act like adults. Children will act the part of grown-ups to perfection while told to do so under hypnosis.

CELEBRITY IMPERSONATION

When told by the hypnotist that they are great movie stars, sports personalities, singers, or politicians, they impersonate the characters suggested to the best of their ability. Often the acting out of the character is truly first rate. As a politician he will give a speech you suggest. As a singer he will sing a popular song he knows. Put the proper music behind him and you'll get a performance.

Any person can be cured of bashfulness or stage fright immediately while hypnotized. Incorrigible children can be made very pleasant by the use of posthypnotic suggestion.

NO WEAKENING OF THE WILL

Some people claim that hypnotism weakens the will. This is absolutely untrue. A subject is naturally more responsive to the hypnotist because of a deep rooted idea that he must follow the operator's suggestions on command. But no weakening of the will occurs. In fact, hypnosis can make the person stronger willed!

If you are working with a subject who feels that he is too susceptible to hypnotic influence, put the person into hypnosis and suggest that he can only be hypnotized upon his own request. Tell him that the one he has most confidence in is himself, and that he is the personal director of all he does, as is his wish.

AWAKENING SOMEONE ELSE'S SUBJECT

If you should ever be called upon to awaken a subject someone else has hypnotized but failed to arouse, go about it in this way: Rehypnotize the subject while he is still in trance until you reach a stage where he will answer your questions or respond to performing some action you suggest. In this way, you will get in rapport with him and it will be an easy manner to arouse him.

The only reason a subject sometimes refuses to come out of hypnosis at the moment suggested is because he enjoys being in the stress free state of hypnosis so much that he is loath to come back to the outside world.

Tell such a subject that unless he snaps out of it quickly now, he will never again be able to enter hypnosis. He will awaken instantly.

FINALLY ...

Here are two, great "suggestion formulae" for you to use; one that increases hypnotic responsiveness, and another for appreciating living life fully to the hilt. Use #1 after hypnotizing a subject and before you commence any experiment:

> #1. *"Everything .. we .. do .. together .. is .. in .. perfect .. harmony .. between .. us, .. and .. it .. gives .. you .. the .. greatest .. pleasure .. to .. go .. into .. profound .. hypnosis, .. and .. perform .. to .. perfection .. everything .. that .. I .. suggest .. you .. perform."*

This harmonizing suggestion forms a background for all hypnotic proceedings the subject will experience, motivating him towards profound hypnosis.

And on arousing a subject from hypnosis, use #2. Suggest:

> #2. *"When .. you .. awaken .. from .. hypnosis .. and .. come .. back .. to .. the .. here .. and .. now, .. you .. will .. be .. in .. love .. with .. the .. total .. of .. Existence .. and .. will .. appreciate .. the .. miracle .. that .. you .. are."*

Awakening from hypnosis with that suggestion embedded in the subconscious is truly miraculous.

College student hypnotized by Tom Silver to think he is rock singer, Bruce Springsteen, singing "Born In The USA". November 1988

170

CHAPTER TWENTY-EIGHT

EXTRA BONUS QUESTIONS AND ANSWERS TO THE HOW-TO BOOK OF HYPNOTISM

ARE PEOPLE NOW ACCEPTING HYPNOSIS?

We think that hypnotherapy is gaining international acceptance and is being utilized by thousands of medical practitioners, psychotherapists, psychologists, and psychiatrists because hypnosis is a science of the mind, and it works.

In the 1700s and 1800s, hypnosis was practiced by some of the top medical Doctors in Europe. Thousands of people were helped and even cured from emotional and physical ailments through the practice of hypnotherapy. Back in those days, the science was called magnetism and mesmerism. Since the mind is now being proven to be a haven of revitalizing chemicals produced in the brain, hypnosis is being used to activate these chemicals in the brain and the positive emotions in the subconscious to help heal and help people to enjoy living life more to the fullest. Hypnosis is not a cure for everything but it sure can help enhance the quality of life, health and happiness.

Hypnosis is becoming the number one form of mental health therapy and is helpful in healing the physical body pains that are created by emotional manifestations in the mind. A physical manifestation of an emotional anxiety is what hypnosis can help relieve. Hypnosis can also produce a chemical balance in the mind by creating and activating chemicals such as seratonin. We will see the science of hypnotism being used more and more every day.

WHAT DO DOCTORS THINK ABOUT HYPNOSIS?

Medical Doctors are now really starting to accept hypnosis and hypnotherapy as a therapeutic tool, which can be utilized in combination with traditional medicine. Medical Doctors say that over 60% of our physical problems stem from our mind. Medical Doctors also say that stress, tension, anxiety, and worry are the biggest factors in the increase of heart attacks and even death in our American culture. These are all emotions, and negative emotions can affect our health, our body and our life. All emotions come from the subconscious mind and can be altered, neutralized or changed through the practice and use of hypnotherapy.

DOES HYPNOSIS CHANGE BRAIN WAVE ACTIVITY?

Yes indeed, our conscious brain wave activity, beats, or cycles do change from our waking state on into the different hypnotic states. The brain wave patterns change as the different depths of hypnotic relaxation occurs. As a person goes deeper into hypnosis, the cycles of brain wave activity get slower and conscious brain wave activity is reduced.

In our waking state of brain wave activity which we call Beta, our conscious brain wave pattern, beats or cycles might range from about 14 to 30 beats or cycles per second. At that stage of conscious brain activity, our conscious or cognitive mind, our what we might call, our waking state of mind is very active and alert. This stage of consciousness occurs during the day.

The second stage of brain wave activity is called Alpha. In Alpha, which is a state of light hypnosis or physical relaxation and restfulness, our brain wave pattern or cycles slow down to about 7 to 13 beats or cycles per second. Light sleep can be considered Alpha.

The next deeper level or stage of hypnosis is called Theta. In the state of Theta, our conscious brain wave activity slows down even more, and would register on a brain wave scanning device at about 4 to about 6 beats or cycles per second. When a person falls into a very deep natural sleep at night, they are probably in the state of "Theta".

The deepest depth of hypnosis is called Delta, or Somnambulism. In Delta, our conscious brain wave activity is reduced to only about 0.1 to about 4 beats or cycles per second. The deeper the level of hypnotic depth, the more unconscious the conscious mind becomes. When the conscious mind becomes restful, quiet, and silent, the subconscious mind becomes responsive and open to accept positive suggestions and emotions. Brain wave cycle beats can vary depending on equipment and technicians.

WHAT ARE THE DIFFERENT STAGES OF HYPNOSIS?

In modern hypnosis most theorists believe that there are three major stages of hypnosis. Some terms used to describe these stages are the Hypnoidal, or light stage. Cataleptic, which could also be called the medium or middle stage of hypnosis, and Somnambulism which is considered the deepest stage of hypnosis.

Some hypnotists believe that there is also a fourth level or depth of hypnosis which they consider the psychic or medium state. In this deep hypnotic depth, E.S.P. and other psychic phenomena might occur. Maybe past life regression also occurs in this deeper level of hypnosis. More research is needed.

Relating to brain wave science. The Hypnoidal or light depth of hypnosis could be considered the state of Alpha. The Cataleptic depth of hypnosis could be considered the state of Theta, and deepest stage of hypnosis, which we call Somnambulism, could also be called the state of Delta.

IS HYPNOTHERAPY SESSIONS EFFECTIVE IN ALL DIFFERENT STAGES, OR HYPNOTIC DEPTHS?

Hypnotherapy sessions to help people overcome negative emotions and health issues can be just as effective on a person who might be in a light stage of hypnosis, as it might be on a person who is deeply hypnotized. Under light, medium, and deep hypnosis, positive suggestions, can be effectively transmitted by the hypnotherapist to the client.
Only fifteen percent of the population will go into the deeper stages of hypnosis on their first time being hypnotized.

Our brain also produces certain mind chemicals under hypnosis or deep physical relaxation that can help to heal our mind and body. Seratonin, Mellatonin, Dopamine, Beta-Endorphins, and more. These chemicals in the brain are stimulated and produced naturally while a person is under hypnosis. That is why so many people feel so refreshed and energized after they awaken from a hypnotherapy session. Fifteen minutes of a hypnotic sleep, is equal to about five or six hours of a natural sleep.

These "mind chemicals" can help to heal mental stress and tensions as well as help to heal some physical pains that can occur from mental negative emotions. These are called body syndromes, which are physical manifestations of an emotional anxiety. These emotions are negative emotions and are located in our subconscious mind.

Hypnotherapy can be beneficial in all stages or depths of hypnosis. In deep hypnosis, somnambulism or delta, regression therapy can occur, where you can regress a person back to anytime period in their current life to help them overcome an event that has created ill health or mental disturbance. Past life regression therapy can also be achieved under the deepest stage of hypnosis.

For entertainment purposes with hypnotism, this depth of conscious silence can bring about illusion and even hallucinations in hypnotized subjects for the purposes of conducting stage hypnotism demonstrations. Some people like I have mentioned before believe that E.S.P. abilities might also become active in a person while under the deepest stage of hypnosis, but that is just an opinion and of course, not a fact.

WHEN DO OUR MINDS START OPERATING?

The subconscious mind is formed and starts developing right after birth and some people think even in the womb before birth. It is located in the medulla oblongata or what is called the inner part of our brain.

From birth to about 3 years of age, everything that goes into a child's life goes directly into their subconscious mind or bio computer. The subconscious absorbs pictures, words, actions, tones and frequencies of the human voice and occurrences in the environment. It is like a sponge absorbs water. The most penetrating experiences are the emotions that are programmed or recorded into the subconscious mind. We are largely influenced and programmed subconsciously by our parents or primary caregivers.

Children record subconsciously from birth, "positive and negatives" message units or emotions from their parents, from other children, from the environment and from animals, like a small child, or baby frightened by a dog.

Some children are filled with positive emotions such as love, trust, security, confidence, understanding, happiness and so fourth. Some children are given negative emotions, words and pictures from their primary care givers or parents of anger, fear, confusion, self-doubt, loneliness, pain, gilt, and other negative emotions, which will become deeply recorded into that child's subconscious mind.

Most people are programmed with a combination of both positive and negative emotions. Negative emotions might create really bad problems in your adult life, because once they are recorded in your subconscious mind, they will always haunt you, and they will be with you for the rest of your life, unless your subconscious mind let's go of them, and releases them through hypnotherapy, or by utilizing some other type of subconscious therapeutic procedure.

Positive emotions if programmed into your subconscious mind, will help you to enjoy life more, and to be healthy, and to have success in your life. Most of us have a limited life script because of the negative emotions that are programmed into our subconscious bio-computer, which creates of dysfunctional bio-computer and a limited mind.

At about 3 years old, a child's conscious mind begins to become activated. That is our logic and reason part of our brain and is only about 10% of our total brain power.
It is actually our tiny bio-computer.

The conscious mind is located in the cortex of our brain or the outer part of the brain. The conscious mind is our cognitive or intellectual part of our mental power. Most people relay only on that part of their brain to succeed without realizing that to have 100 percent of total mental power, both of your minds need to be working together.

When our conscious mind is formed, we create a barrier between our conscious and subconscious mind, which can be called a critical factor or critical area of mind. When you are in a hypnotized state by a hypnotherapist, or by the environment, such as by watching movies or television, the critical factor or barrier between your conscious mind, and subconscious mind, opens up, and you are then in a hypnotic receptive state which can then record or activate positive or negative emotions. The movie "Jaws" hypnotized the viewers in the movie theaters and thousands of people all over the world had fears of the ocean and of sharks. Hypnosis is all around us in the environment.

Driving a car on automatic pilot and thinking thoughts of the day. Driving while day dreaming and then wondering how did I arrive at my destination, or was I going the right speed. When you first learned how to drive, the pattern and program of driving an automobile had been recorded or embedded into your subconscious mind. The suggestions and patterns of driving were stimulated by your emotions of wanting to drive. Therefore you can for the most part drive and think thoughts because the pattern of driving has been recorded into your strong bio-computer, your subconscious mind. When your conscious mind is active is usually when children our taught logical information in the schools. In America it is around the first grade. Now our subconscious continuously operates with our conscious mind.

When our conscious mind is operating, so is our subconscious mind operating by identifying and associating with our conscious thoughts. The subconscious, mind "Identifies and Associates" with the conscious mind thoughts. We are continuously bringing up thoughts, pictures, words and emotions from our subconscious mind. Those emotions and pictures and words are either helping us or hurting us.

If you have ever over reacted to a situation and looked back and wondered to yourself, why did you get so upset, it was because your subconscious mind identified that situation that was making you angry with a past experience and emotion of anger. The subconscious instantly related your conscious mind thoughts to the subconscious mind emotions. Both of your minds are on automatic operation during your waking state of life activity.

We are not talking about the theory of right or left-brain, since this author's hypnotic opinion is that we have an outer and inner brain function. Two mental bio- computers, that are either working together in harmony, or they are in discord, and in a dysfunctional state of limitation.

Our subconscious mind never sleeps. In a receptive hypnotic state, the subconscious records, retains, and freely accepts emotions, pictures, words and thoughts. It is receiving or imputing data. In a natural sleep like the one each and every one of us does every night. The subconscious in transmitting thoughts, emotions, pictures, words in the form of dreams.

WHAT IS ENVIRONMENTAL HYPNOSIS?

Environmental hypnosis is the process of being hypnotized by the environment. Like I had mentioned earlier, driving your car and day dreaming you are hypnotized.

When you learned how to drive the pattern of driving got accepted and recorded into your subconscious mind and when you, day dream, your subconscious is driving for you.

Watching a movie we become hypnotized into the movie and feel the effects of the movie. We start to kind of live and feel the emotions of the movie. If the movie is sad, people cry, if it s happy or exciting people are going through the roller coaster of emotions. As I had also mentioned earlier, about the movie Jaws. That movie created lots of fear in people after watching it, because it activated a fear emotion in the subconscious mind. The horror movies depicting violence have helped create more insensitivity to human life, and people are now committing more crimes than ever before. The negative emotional movies do affect your life.

Movies put you into a hypnotized state of mind and movies can produce good happy feelings, or movies can activate fear, hatred, violence and other negative images and patterns. Be careful what movies you let your children watch and be careful what movies you watch.

You can be hypnotized many different times a day. Listening to music, watching a soap opera, watching a sports event, working, shopping in a super market, smelling a good smell to name a few. We go into hypnosis and magnified concentration all the time, every day without even knowing that we are hypnotized by the environment.

CAN WATCHING A MOVIE HYPNOTIZE YOU?

Like I have mentioned earlier, movies can create good positive feelings and movies can also activate subconscious fears, anxieties, and other negative emotions. Children who watched the Friday the 13th movies had fears of going to sleep after watching that movie, because the fear of being killed in their sleep was accepted into the emotions in the subconscious mind. The movie jaws created fears of sharks and water in thousands of people around the world.

CAN READING A BOOK HYPNOTIZE YOU?

Reading a good book and feeling the emotions created by the book and story is hypnotic and can hypnotize you. A good book is always a book that activates your emotions and puts you into hypnosis.

WHAT SAFETY CONSIDERATIONS SHOULD BE TAKEN WHEN CONDUCTING GROUP HYPNOSIS?

Some hypnotists might say that there is no harm at all to anyone who is hypnotized in a large group. We believe that you should always be careful and use good judgment when conducting group hypnosis. The safety of the subjects you are hypnotizing, should be your number one priority.

It is hard to have complete control over the situation when you are conducting hypnosis demonstrations and suggestions on a group of people all at the same time. If you hypnotize a person to show a physical demonstration, you want to make sure that the people you are hypnotizing, prior to being hypnotized has no physical problems or if you are hypnotizing females in a group, please make sure that none of the female volunteers are pregnant.

You do not want to harm or physically hurt anyone. You want to use good judgment and always give positive good healthy suggestions to benefit the subjects, and not to harm them. You also want to make sure that the area where you are hypnotizing your subjects and volunteer's, is safe so that no body falls, or hurts themselves. Personal Liability insurance for stage hypnotism performers is recommended.

CAN A PERSON PERFORM SUPER HUMAN FEATS WHILE HYPNOTIZED?

People have been known to show extra ordinary strength and performance abilities under hypnosis. Controlled breathing and the reduction of air intake under hypnosis can also be performed. Even total pain control has also been demonstrated with people under hypnosis.

WHAT ARE DREAMS AND WHAT DO THEY MEAN?

We usually go through three different stages of dreaming at night. Precognitive Dreams, Wishful Thinking Dreams, and Venting Dreams. Precognitive dreaming is creative idea dreaming. Wishful thinking dreaming is dreams of goals or aspirations that you have in life. The last dream cycle is called, venting dreams, which usually occur a few hours or so before you wake up. Venting dreams are the dreams that you have, to let go of previous days emotions or activity. Events from your past such, as traumatic events or major emotional situations that might have affected you might be trying to be released or vented out in the forms of dreams. If you keep having the same dream over and over again, that dream might be a subconscious anxiety that you for some reason cannot release out of your mind.

Even under anesthesia in a hospital with a patient being operated on by a doctor, that patient's conscious mind might be asleep, but his subconscious mind is still very much awake and hearing and even responding to the words or actions of the people around him.

WHAT IS REINCARNATION?

Reincarnation is not directly connected with the study of hypnosis other than that of a popular form of hypnotherapy that has developed over the years, and is known as "Past Life Regression Therapy." In this process, the subject is hypnotized and told to go back in time to a time when he/she lived prior to their current lifetime. Often fascinating stories are revealed, which frequently benefit the person in this lifetime.

Reincarnation is really the evolution of the soul, and implies that we live lifetime after lifetime in renewed body after renewed body. Some say the "stories" produced from out of the subconscious are pure fantasies, much like dreams, while others take them as factual experiences lived through in a previous life. And the third kind of opinion on this topic is that "we can't confirm or deny this yet."

Whatever, the fact remains that this form of hypnotherapy has helped many people.

IS REINCARNATION TRUE?

Current Western theology does not accept it. Eastern theology has no question about it at all, and reverently states, "It is the way and every moment something within us dies and is renewed, and life goes on".

"It is the way of the Universe." We are safe in saying that more than half the world believes in reincarnation as factual truth.

Strictly speaking, the Christian religion believes in reincarnation too. And it is the very foundation of that religion -- the second coming of Jesus Christ. "And all believers will join Him in heaven." This is a form of reincarnation -- only once. However, the Oriental believes in multiple lives of the soul. All of these religions, no matter whether a single reincarnation or multiple reincarnations, derived themselves from a common concept of the ancient Egyptian belief -- the Soul is immortal.

WHAT CAN BE LEARNED FROM PAST LIFE EXPERIENCES AND MEMORIES?

If it is so, we learn that death is the greatest lie in the world, and that we are immortal. That what we call "death" is but a transition from one existence to another -- like the passing from one room to another room. And each lifetime after each lifetime is a school of experiences in which the evolution of the soul (our real SELF) learns and grows in a perpetual expansion of consciousness.

IS A REINCARNATION MEMORY OR EXPERIENCE UNDER HYPNOSIS ALWAYS REAL?

It all depends on whether one believes in the existence of past lives or not. To the subject who believes so, or who experienced such, the past life can be so "real" that he/she is a true believer. Countless extremely interesting past life stories can be the best candidates for novel or movies. So, in this sense, to the subject, it is real, or even "very real" to him or her. However, to others, these experiences may be just fantasies.

A past life memory regression might be a real experience or it can be something else. Not everybody believes that they have lived before and there still is no actual proof that we have lived lives before our current one, but there seems to be more and more people who are becoming open to the idea of past life memories. More therapists are utilizing past life memory regression as a therapeutic tool in helping a person overcome a negative emotion or habit.

WHAT OTHER THINGS BESIDES A PAST LIFE COULD THE REINCARNATION EXPERIENCE REPRESENT?

From our point of view, "A Past Life Regression" is just one of many methods used in hypnotherapy. Whether it is real or not is not our concern. If a subject believes on such and can be benefited by, there is no reason why we could not use this type of therapy.

Also, in our experiences of more than several thousands of "Past Life Regression", we have always asked the question right before a subject leave a "past life" memory, "What have you learned from this life?" The answer to this question is very useful. The answers usually are very heart-touching, such as "Love thy family", "To be Kind", "Give to others", etc. Therefore, we think the most valuable thing about the past life experience, is what the subject can learn from a past life and use that wisdom in his or her current life.

Past life memories can be a number of different things. It might be pure fantasy. It might be a real past life memory that has surfaced up from the subconscious mind. A past life memory might also be a story or a metaphor of a past life that is not a real life but represents the present fear or anxiety that a client is trying to overcome. In other words, it can be a created or imagined past life trauma. A memory of drowning in the ocean in a past life might also be a childhood fear created by a boating accident when the person was quite young. Maybe a past life memory might also be a opened up frequency in the human brain that is receiving a single or message of a past life that might not even belong to the person experiencing the past life. To a therapist, the regression therapy might help to neutralize or resolve a inner mental conflict, wall or barrier that is holding a person back from living life to the fullest.

HOW CAN YOU BE SURE THAT YOU HAVE HAD A TRUE PAST LIFE EXPERIENCE UNDER HYPNOSIS?

Frankly, we can't. Trying to prove or disprove any given past life is impossible and impractical. However, as long as we keep in mind that "Past Life Regression" is one of many hypnotherapy tools and we use it appropriately, it doesn't matter if past life memories are real or not real. That answer is still in debate. There is no actual proof of you having a real past life experience, unless we guess if you can go back to that past life place and find the facts about that life to see if they match your past life memory.

DOES OUR SUBCONSCIOUS MIND EVER SLEEP?

Our subconscious mind never sleeps, and in fact it is always active and operating. Even under anesthesia in a hospital with patient being operated on by a doctor, that patients conscious mind might be a sleep, but his subconscious mind is still very much awake and hearing and even responding to the words and actions of the people around him in the operating room.

CAN WE CONTROL OUR CONSCIOUS MIND?

Our conscious mental computer is our logic and reason part of our brain, and is also our will power and is the weakest part of our brain power, while our subconscious mind is our emotional, conditioned, habit and pattern part of our mental computer. It is the strongest and most powerful part of our brain-power and mind. It must operate for you properly and positively, and in sync with your conscious mind in order for you to reach all your goals in life. If your conscious mind or your inner talking voice gives yourself negative words or suggestions, you will never achieve true mental power. You cannot be happy if you consciously and logically punish yourself everyday by thinking negative thoughts.

You must exercise your conscious mind to think positive thoughts, emotions and words, that you want your subconscious mind to respond to. You want your subconscious mind to respond to only positive emotions, by giving yourself positive suggestions everyday. "I'm happy, I live life to the fullest, I love myself, I am confident in every thing I do, I have lot's of energy", etc. Both of your bio mental computers need to be functioning properly and under your operation because you are the operator of your mind, thoughts, and action. You can tell your mind when to think and what to think because you are really the master of your mind. You have to start being in control of both of your bio computers, and make them work for you. Make both of your minds (conscious and subconscious), work for **"You"** starting right now!

"YOU DESERVE THE BEST OF EVERYTHING!"

185

Tom Silver holding the "Gold Plate" of honor presented to him from the
Taiwan "Department of Defense" for his work with
"Forensic Hypnosis" and "Memory Activation"
July 1997

Tom Silver "Master of Hypnosis" and his Chinese Interpreter,
Mr. Timothy Huang, Performing the astonishing demonstration of
"Interlingual Hypnotic Trance Induction" by Hypnotizing Miss. China
live on the Taiwan National Television Show "Super Sunday".
Miss China is being hypnotized with Interlingual Hypnosis in her own
native language of Mandarin Chinese, and taken to a past life.

CHAPTER TWENTY-NINE

INTERLINGUAL HYPNOTIC TRANCE INDUCTION
Created and Copyright in 1994 by Tom Silver
Master Hypnotherapist & Re-Educator

This chapter deals with the art, science and practice of a method of hypnotizing people who do not speak the same language that you may speak. Most hypnotherapists or stage hypnosis performers have only practiced hypnosis or hypnotherapy on people who speak the same language as the hypnotherapist. An example of this might be an English-speaking hypnotist who hypnotizes people in the language of English. Many people who practice the art of hypnotism even think that it is impossible to hypnotize a person in a foreign language.

In 1994 in Taipei Taiwan (Republic of China) I was able to create a formula and method to hypnotize the people of Taiwan through an interpreter in Mandarin Chinese who was not a hypnotist, but just a person who spoke both Mandarin Chinese and English. During my six years of hard work in introducing the Taiwan culture to the science of hypnotism and the utilization of forensic hypnosis for investigation purposes for memory activation, I worked hard on perfecting my method of Translingual Hypnotism.

I am proud to say that the over Five Thousand Year Old Chinese Culture, the Taiwan Department of Defense, and the people of Taiwan would never have recognized the science of hypnotism or awarded me a "Gold Plate of Honor" in July of 1997, from the Taiwan Minister of Defense had I not been able to hypnotize people in a foreign language.

Hypnosis is becoming recognized and utilized world wide now for therapy and even in conjunction with standard medical practices. Medical doctors are even learning more about the applications of hypnosis. With the ever growing demand for hypnotists around the world, the science and application of being able to hypnotize people through an interpreter is a system and technique that is important to all hypnotherapists.

I would like to thank Mr. Timothy Huang of Taipei Taiwan, for being my interpreter, my friend, and the key person in helping me introduce the amazing science of hypnotism to the Taiwan Culture and the people of Taiwan. Tim Huang has since become a hypnotherapist with a practice in Taipei. Tim and I have created a working Hypnosis Research Center in Taiwan with two other hypnotherpists/researchers to help further the scientific development of hypnotism in Taiwan, as well as to help create acceptance of this science by the medical and mental practitioners of Taiwan and all of Asia. Our research center is also developing more accurate methods of hypnotic inductions and suggestive formulas. I am proud to say that through hypnotherapy, I have helped thousands of people in Taiwan, including children, teenagers and adults become more confident in themselves, and to acquire greater health and happiness.

More people than ever before are suffering from mental illness and negative emotions. Medical Doctors say that stress, tension, worry and anger kill's more Americans than anything else, including cancer. People in the United States and in other countries commit suicide or harm other people because of the negative thoughts they think and emotions they create. More Children then ever before suffer from depression, sleep depravation, fears, angers and some of the same negative emotions and habits that adults have. When I was in Taiwan I read newspaper articles of children in Taiwan and Japan taking their own lives because the pressures in their lives were too much to bear. Hypnotherapy is a Universal science that can help people all over the world and with the utilization of Interlingual Hypnotism, all language boundaries and limitations are now gone. You can hypnotize people through interpreters.

I will now give you some answers to some of the most asked questions about Interlingual Hypnotism. These answers will help to give you a better understanding of what it is, and how it works. I will also give you some wonderful knowledge and insight on how to hypnotize people who speak a different language.

The information that I will give you, will only be effective and will work for you, if you practice and if you are patient. I practiced for days and weeks on perfecting my methods to hypnotize people in Taiwan, through an Interpreter speaking Mandarin Chinese. My method works!

SOME QUESTIONS AND ANSWERS ABOUT "INTERLINGUAL HYPNOTIC TRANCE INDUCTION"!

WHAT IS THE INTERLINUAL HYPNOTIC TRANCE INDUCTION METHOD?

Interlingual Hypnotic Trance Induction, is the method or formula of hypnotizing a person through an Interpreter or another person who is speaking the subjects or person who is being hypnotized "Primary or Native Language".

The word Inter-Lingual relates to more than one language. Such as using the English language and using the Mandarin Chinese language combined together to hypnotize a person.

CAN AN INTERPRETER HYPNOTIZE A PERSON?

A hypnotist is the person who hypnotizes the clients or subjects, and an interpreter is the person, who assist's the hypnotist, by using or speaking the subject's primary language. The interpreter is the hypnotist's assistant and not the actual person hypnotizing the subject. A hypnotist who is able to speak more than one language can always hypnotize a person in that language even if it is not the hypnotist's primary language.

HOW EFFECTIVE IS INTER-LINGUAL HYPNOSIS?

Interlingual hypnosis is just as effective in hypnotizing a person just as any other type of hypnosis process or induction. As long as the pacing, and timing are conducted in a successful manner by the hypnotist and interpreter, the induction of hypnotism will be successful. Sometimes Interlingual Hypnotic Trance Induction can be even more effective by creating what I call, "The misdirection of the Conscious Mind".

This procedure is performed with a hypnosis induction in which the hypnotherapist, creates an overloading process of the subject or client's conscious mind though words, suggestions, and misdirection/confusion and then instantly through a "Shock Induction" technique, converting that "Peak of Conscious Mind Activity" into a deep hypnotic or delta stage of conscious sleep.

This hypnosis technique, "should" only be conducted by trained and experienced Clinical Hypnotherapists.

191

WHAT SPECIAL CONSIDERATIONS SHOULD BE TAKEN INTO CONSIDERATION IN CONDUCTING INTERLINGUAL HYPNOSIS?

The most important consideration taken into account when conducting a "Interlingual Hypnotic Trance Induction" method or for hypnotizing people, is the correct interpretation of the words that the hypnotist is using to hypnotize the subject. The Interpreter should know exactly every meaning of each and every word that the hypnotist is trying to communicate to the subject, or else the wrong meaning and messages that the hypnotist is telling the subject will be confusing and will have negative affects on the hypnotic induction and therapy or suggestions.

The pacing and timing of the hypnotist and interpreter are also important. It must be smooth and skillfully conducted. The speaking pattern of both the hypnotist and the Interpreter are important and should match or complement each other instead of conflict and clash with each other.

HOW DEEPLY HYPNOTIZED CAN A PERSON BECOME WITH INTERLINGUAL HYPNOSIS?

A person can go just as deep into hypnosis as with any other hypnosis type of induction.
All the way down to Delta or what is call Somnambulism.

WHAT HYPNOTIC DEMONSTRATIONS OR POSITIVE CHANGES CAN OCCUR WITH INTERLINGUAL HYPNOTIC TRANCE INDUCTION?

With the application of Interlingual Hypnotic Trance Induction, everything that can occur with the traditional forms of hypnosis and hypnotherapy can also occur with

Translingual Hypnotism. With Interlingual Hypnotism, you can help a person to lose weight, stop smoking, increase motivation and confidence, reduce stress, tensions and worries, increase memory retention and focus and concentration, become a better athlete and elevate a persons level of success by increasing the positive emotions in a persons subconscious mind. Interlingual Hypnotic Trance Induction hypnotherapy can be used for natural childbirth, for surgery to reduce pain, for depression ,to reduce fear and more. Translingual hypnosis demonstrations can also show pure creativity and imagination suggestions for live Hypnosis show demonstrations. The subconscious mind does not distinguish between fantasy and reality. If the subconscious mind can accept a suggestion of creativity or imagination, then the subconscious mind can also accept positive suggestion to help change a person life, or to increase the physical health of a person.

HOW MANY PEOPLE CAN BE HYPNOTIZED AT ONCE WITH INLINGUAL HYPNOTIC TRANCE INDUCTION?

In February of 1995, Timothy Huang and myself hypnotized approximately 3800 people all at the same time through an Interpreter in Mandarin Chinese. This was the very first Interlingual Hypnosis World's Record. Groups of people can all be hypnotized to one degree or another. Everybody's depth of hypnosis may vary, but some people in a crowd will go into very deep levels of hypnosis. Take for example a famous celebrity, or musical artists such as "The Beatles", or even a dynamic political speaker. They can hypnotize you into a very receptive state of emotional concentration without the you even knowing that you are hypnotized. Movies can hypnotize you and activate or create positive or negative emotions or feelings from your subconscious mind. When you watch the movie, the emotions created by the movie will automatically and without thinking, come up to your conscious mind by-passing your logic and reason, giving you feelings of feeling good, sad, happy, mad, angry, fearful and more. I can remember one movie that made millions of people afraid of sharks and the ocean. Movies are hypnotizing.

CAN CHILDREN BE HYPNOTIZED BY USING THIS METHOD OF TRANLINGUAL HYPNOTISM?

Yes! Children can certainly be hypnotized by an interpreter by using the same hypnosis induction methods that you would use on children who speak English as their primary language.

WHO MAKES THE BEST INTERPRETER?

Anybody who speaks two languages can make a good interpreter for Interlingual hypnotism, however, the better that the interpreter speaks and understands your own primary language, the better co-hypnotist he/she will be. The better their understanding of what they are interpreting, the better word translations can be used for the subject to follow and understand in order to hypnotize the subject and to implant positive hypnosis suggestions.

If you are working with a child and one of the parents can speak your language and the child's primary language, they would probably make the best candidate to use as the interpreter and person to help you to hypnotize that child. The more comfortable and safe and secure you make the child in this situation, the better the chance of inducing a deeper state of hypnosis for the therapy.

Now we will discuss the method formula that is needed in order to hypnotize people is another language. In order to successfully complete a deep hypnotic induction on a subject through an interpreter, it is important to:

FIND AN INTERPRETER WHO SPEAKS AND COMPREHENDS YOUR LANGUAGE WELL ENOUGH TO TRANSLATE YOUR WORDS AND SUGGESTIONS TO THE SUBJECT WITH THEIR CORRECT MEANING.

An example of this might be the word "**sleep**". To the average English speaking person, the word "sleep" would probably mean, when we are asleep, such as a night in our beds. Now to the hypnotist, the word "sleep" means to enter into a hypnotic sleep, not a natural sleep. Now the word sleep in another language might mean the same thing, or maybe something entirely different.

When I first worked with an interpreter and hypnotized some subjects, I said to the subject the word "sleep" and when it was translated into the Mandarin language, the person just stood there as if they were frozen solid. I asked a person in the room, what word did the interpreter say in Mandarin Chinese, and what did that word mean, and the person said that the interpreter said a word that meant to "Freeze", as if to not move instead of sleep.

THE PROPER MEANING OF THE WORDS AND THE CORRECT INTERPRETATION OF THE WORDS THAT ARE TRANSLATED INTO ANOTHER LANGUAGE MUST BE INTERPRETED CORRECTLY.

Explain to the interpreter what hypnosis is, and how hypnosis works. The more understanding of the induction process and science of hypnotism, the better the interpreter will be in helping you to hypnotize a subject. Maybe even showing examples on video or even demonstrating what a person might look like when they are physically relaxed and in a hypnotic state of relaxation might be beneficial.

THE TIMING AND PACING OF THE WORDS OF THE HYPNOTIST AND INTERPRETER MUST BE SMOOTH AND SHOULD NEVER OVERLAP EACH OTHER.

When conducting a hypnosis or hypnotherapy session with a client through an interpreter in another language, it is important to make sure that there is a smooth transition from each language without overlapping, or to long of a space or rest between languages. If you and a interpreter practice together, you can create a type of rhythm of your words together and even be able to almost mirror your voices together with emotional vocal expressions, which will create more of a successful hypnosis session.

ALWAYS EXPLAIN TO THE CLIENT OR SUBJECT BEFORE YOU HYPNOTIZE THEM, EXACTLY HOW YOU ARE GOING TO HYPNOTIZE THEM.

Before you hypnotize your subject or client through an interpreter in a foreign language, you should always explain to your subject, exactly what is going to happen to them physically when you hypnotize them. The directions of how you will hypnotize them, will act as a pre-hypnotic suggestion for them to follow, and that will help you to hypnotize the subject easier and quicker.

With directions to follow, the fears of the unknown of "what's going to happen to me" are gone, and so this method will lessen the subject's resistance to being hypnotized. The mind likes to follow directions.

An example of this type of pre-hypnosis induction would be as follows:

"In a moment, I will ask you to close your eyes, when you do, you will enter into a hypnotic sleep. Your head will drop down and rest and relax and your whole body will become relaxed. When I touch you on your shoulder, you will open your eyes and look into my eyes. I will then look into your eyes and say the word sleep! Your eyes will close. Your head will drop down. Your body will instantly relax, and you will enter into a deep hypnotic sleep. Do you understand me?" And get a yes or nod of the head.
Then say to the subject, "Okay, I will now hypnotize you." After that, you simply start your hypnosis formula and induction, and do exactly as you told the subject you would do, and they will enter into a wonderfully deep state of hypnosis.

Remember when conducting translingual hypnotism, that you are speaking only a few words at a time, and then pausing for your interpreter to translate and speak the words in the subjects own language. .

In a moment (pause), now the interpreter says the in the subjects language, and then you continue with the sentence. I will ask you to close your eyes, (pause) interpreter speaks and then you continue, and so forth.

LITERAL SUGGESTIONS, WHICH ARE SIMPLIFIED SUGGESTIONS TO THE HYPNOTIZED SUBJECT IN TRANSLINGUAL HYPNOTISM WORKS THE BEST.

You never want to get too complicated or confusing in your hypnosis induction or hypnotherapy sessions with trans-lingual hypnosis, because you will only confuse your interpreter and subject, and will cloud up the positive simple literal suggestions that will be much more easily accepted. The subconscious mind understands simple directions better than confusing directions. The conscious mind uses logic and reason and is the intellectual part of the mind. The more direct and easier you present positive suggestions to the subconscious mind of the translingual hypnotized subject, the quicker and more effectively they will be accepted. This simple rule will give you greater success with your clients.

PRACTICE, PRACTICE, PRACTICE, AND YOU WILL BE ABLE TO HYPNOTIZE A PERSON THROUGH AN INTERPRETER IN A FOREIGN LANGUAGE.

The more that you can practice with an interpreter, the better of a team of players you will be as your interpreter is actually your co-hypnotherapist and partner, when it comes to hypnotizing your subjects or clients.

The more you practice together, the better harmonization between your voices, words and sentences will be obtained, and the more your two voices will sound and even become like one voice.

You now have some wonderful knowledge and insight about the science of hypnotism, because you have just read the HOW-TO BOOK OF HYPNOTISM. You will now be able to perform many amazing things. Your imagination can be your guide as to what you can and will accomplish.

A knowledge of hypnotism is valuable to everyone. It brings an appreciation of how wonderful an instrument our human mind truly is. You literally have a biocomputer inside your head, in which a knowledge of hypnotism can show you how to operate this amazing and unbelievably powerful bio-computer, your subconscious mind!

INTERLINGUAL HYPNOTIC TRANCE INDUCTION!
Tom Silver Hypnotizing 3800 People at the same time through an
Interpreter in Mandarin Chinese.

199

Hypnotically How-To Do What We Do.
Ormond McGill and Tom Silver. 2001

ABOUT THE AUTHORS

Ormond McGill is a name with which to conjure to those who know mystery. He is known as the "Dean of American Hypnotists", and as a magician and hypnotist of international reputation has toured in many parts of the World with his exciting stage shows: "East Indian Miracles," "Mental-Magic", and the "Concert of Hypnotism". Ormond McGill is a member of the National Guild of Hypnotists, The International Brotherhood of Magicians and the Society of American Magicians.

In addition, he is also a naturalist of prominence, and his contributions to entomology and conchology being well-known. Among his previously published books are: *The Secret World of Witchcraft*, *Religious Mysteries of the Orient* (co-authored with Ron Ormond), *The Encyclopedia of Genuine Stage Hypnotism*, *The Art of Stage Hypnotism*, *How To Produce Miracles*, and *Entertaining With Magic*.

Tom Silver started the Silver Hypnosis Institute to help teach, train and educate students as well as practicing clinical hypnotherapists on the many methods, formulas and induction techniques he has pioneered over the past 20 years in America and in Taiwan. Tom Silver is a certified Clinical Hypnotherapist with a private practice in Southern California. He is an active member of The National Guild of Hypnotists and The American Counseling Association. He is a master of hypnosis, and Tom Silver has toured the World conducting seminars, lectures, and demonstrations on the scientific and therapeutic values hypnotism. He was one of the first hypnotherapists in the world to create the method of mass-hypnosis through an interpreter in a foreign language.

In February 1995, Tom Silver hypnotized over thirty-eight hundred people at the same time in Taiwan, R.O.C., setting the first "Inter-lingual Hypnosis World's Record".

He hypnotized the entire audience in Mandarin Chinese through an interpreter. Tom Silver was awarded a "Gold Plate Of Honor" from the Taiwan Defense Department in July of 1997 for his work with Forensic Hypnotism and memory activation.

This method of hypnosis Tom Silver created and authored is now classified as "Interlingual Hypnotic Trance Induction" © 1995.

While in Taiwan, Tom Silver lectured about the positive therapeutic values of hypnosis on National Taiwan Television and to the Taiwan Police Academy, members of the Taiwan Olympic Committee, students, professors, doctors and businessmen. He also hypnotized famous celebrities weekly on the #1 most watched television show in Taiwan called "Super Sunday".

Tom Silver has performed hypnosis stage shows for hotels, companies, universities, and corporations throughout the world, including Las Vegas and Ceasar's Palace in Atlantic City, Microsoft Corporation, Hughes Aircraft, Hitachi Corporation, the 3M Corporation, Costco Corporation, Atlantic Richfield, UCLA and Loyola Marymount University, just to name a few.

Tom Silver has helped companies and their employees increase productivity in the workplace, creating a happy, motivated, stress-free environment. Students have also found that Tom Silver's methods CYBERSUGGESTION™ to be very beneficial to help them with memory retention, confidence, focus and concentration.

Tom Silver has appeared and performed live hypnosis demonstrations on such television shows as NBC's "The Other Half" with Dick Clark, The Sally Jesse Rafael Show, TNN's "Ultimate Revenge",

Fox Television Special "Powers of The Paranormal", "Hypnotized", his own CBS television One Hour Special, Comedy Centrals "The Mans Show", the "Montel Williams Show" on UPN, the "Mike & Mattie Show" on ABC, and the "Home and Family Show" on the Family Channel.

Tom has also been performing live on radio since 1990 as the KROQ "Radio Hypnotist" on the "Kevin and Bean Morning Show" in Los Angeles, California and has appeared on many radio stations across the country. Tom Silver is also known as "The NBA Hypnotist" and has performed hypnosis shows for major sports events and playoff games.

Tom Silver's hypnosis stage shows, lectures and seminars are energizing, exciting, fun and inspiring. His abilities as a therapeutic technician and hypnotherapist have helped thousands of people around the world become happier, healthier, and more successful in their lives.

For information on contacting Tom Silver Hypnotherapist, contact the "Silver Hypnosis Institute" at
1 (888) MIND P.W.R. or at www.tomsilver.com.

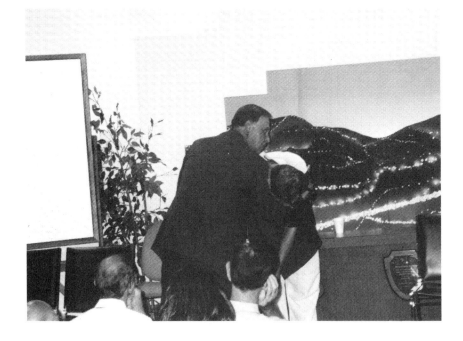